BOOKS BY I. A. HOROWITZ

Chess for Beginners

World Chessmasters in Battle Royal
(WITH HANS KMOCH)

BOOKS BY FRED REINFELD

The Treasury of Chess Lore

The Immortal Games of Capablanca

Winning Chess

The Fireside Book of Chess
(WITH IRVING CHERNEV)

HOW TO THINK AHEAD IN CHESS: *The Methods and Techniques of Planning Your Entire Game*

BY I. A. HOROWITZ AND FRED REINFELD

A Fireside Book Published by **Simon and Schuster**

TENTH PAPERBACK PRINTING

SBN 671-21138-2 FIRESIDE PAPERBACK EDITION

MANUFACTURED IN THE UNITED STATES OF AMERICA

For Lee and Jack

CONTENTS

PART THREE

Playing With the Black Pieces Against 1 P—Q4

PART FOUR

*How to Exploit Inferior Play
by Your Opponent*

INTRODUCTION

Many years ago, the mighty Capablanca engaged in a rough and tumble chess game with a New York expert. Momentarily forgetting that he was invincible, Capa lost!

At this unexpected turn of events, the spectators were amazed. How could the grand master lose to one who was, comparatively, a second-rater?

"How far ahead do you think over the chessboard?" one of them asked the Champion. And, as befitted the titleholder, the impressive reply came back: "Ten moves!"

"How far do *you* think ahead?" the winner of this particular contest was asked. And he replied, "Only one move."

Now here was a confusing state of affairs! How could a chess player who thinks only one move ahead, defeat another who thinks ten moves ahead? The victor then explained: "I think one move ahead—but it is always the best move!"

It is really no great secret that the right move in each position is the sure path to victory. To find the right move invariably, however, is beyond the power of ordinary mortals. What *is* within his grasp, is the right way to think ahead. Not far ahead. Accurate appraisal is more important than deep calculation.

The purpose of this book is to teach *the right way to think ahead*.

It is a common failing of all chess learners to want to become generals before they have no more than an inkling of strategy and tactics. Naturally, when put to the test, they wind up in a welter of confusion. . . . Attack? . . . Defend? . . . Where? . . . When? . . . How? . . . All these are perplexing questions. And they will remain so, until the learner familiarizes himself with guiding principles and patterns.

The ready answers to these questions shape the presentation of this book. It is with these in mind that we urge the learner to familiarize himself with three basic patterns, which will carry him through all the openings that he may encounter in his games. With this fundamental knowledge at his command, the learner is shown how to think ahead by examples from actual play, step-by-step, to the end of the game.

In our zeal to emphasize the strong points of our recommendations, we may leave the impression that White has a forced win and that Black has a forced draw. Definitely, this is not so. Only the astute play of a master, however, can challenge some of the minor conjectures. And this book is not intended for masters!

After you become thoroughly familiar with the patterns of play recommended in this book, you can, if you wish, branch out into other openings. The principles involved in these patterns obtain in all patterns of play.

In the course of reading the book, you will notice references to detailed treatment of the pin, the fork and other tactical techniques. Such detailed treatment does not come within the scope of this book, in which tactical techniques are subordinated to the general problem of over-all planning of your game. But readers who are interested in studying tactical methods will find it useful to consult *Winning Chess.*°

° WINNING CHESS by Irving Chernev and Fred Reinfeld. *Simon and Schuster, New York, 1948.*

♔ PART ONE ♔

Playing With the White Pieces:
Stonewall Pattern

CHAPTER 1

What Opening Shall I Play?

THIS book has been written to show you what to do after the opening stage has been passed. But in order to have a good position for the middle game, you must play the opening well. Hence the question: *"What opening shall I play?"*

Our answer to this question is a very unusual one. Our solution of the problem will doubtless surprise you, but before you have read very far in this book you will, we hope, be delighted with the solution and apply it advantageously in your own games.

The solution is:

With the White pieces, play one standard opening (the Stonewall Variation, discussed in Part I).

With the Black pieces, play one standard defense against 1 P—K4 (the Dragon Variation, discussed in Part II).

Likewise with the Black pieces, play one standard defense against 1 P—Q4 (Lasker's Defense, discussed in Part III).

This is the first book in which such a revolutionary treatment of the chess openings has been advocated for average players. We believe, therefore, that we owe you a brief analysis of the conditions which make it necessary for you to limit your opening repertoire in this drastic manner.

The standard manuals on opening play contain thousands of opening variations, thousands of alternative variations, thousands of annotations!

To try to master this material is obviously a hopeless undertaking. Every year new variations are introduced, old variations are refurbished, popular lines are demolished, while hitherto discredited variations are rehabilitated. Despite their presumably superior knowledge, the masters are by no means united in their opinions as to the best opening variations.

What, then, are you to conclude? ! To assimilate this vast body of knowledge is physically impossible. To ignore it is perilous. Obviously, what is needed is some golden, practicable mean between over-specialization and blithe ignorance.

The sensible middle way is provided by the careful selection of a limited number of satisfactory opening lines. In each case, the recommended line meets the three basic needs of all good opening play:

(1) *effective and rapid development*
(2) *adequate control of the center*
(3) *permanent validity regardless of fluctuations in theory*

In the pages that follow, you will become familiar with these recommended openings. You will study carefully selected games which emphasize the kind of play that results from these openings. By means of photographs and diagrams, you will have impressed on your mind's eye the kind of *visual, repetitive patterns* that characteristically evolve from these openings. You will learn, in unexampled detail, just where each piece and Pawn plays in the opening, and what these forces may be expected to achieve in the ensuing middle game.

Thus you will acquire a knowledge of these openings which will be of inestimable value to you in your own games. In these games of your own, you will be able to direct the play into familiar channels, secure in the realization that you know what to play for, know how to plan, know how to get the most out of a well-played opening. Above all, you will be armored in the confidence that comes from playing a good opening, freed from the handicaps of self-doubt and discouragement.

It will be possible for you to play these openings and defenses at will against almost any opposition: you need not be concerned about the handful of masters who, like as not, select esoteric lines to confuse their less sophisticated opponents. You don't play against these masters; hence you need not worry about their incredibly subtle opening repertoire.

And so, by limiting your study to a mere three openings and defenses, you will be able to concentrate on the really important details. You will not befuddle your brain with extraneous theoretical knowledge, much of which you would never have an opportunity to use in any event.

To come to specific openings: we recommend that when playing with the White pieces you begin 1 P—Q4 with a view to adopting the Stonewall Attack. (Chapters 2, 3, 4 and 5 are devoted to this line of play.)

By playing 1 P—Q4 you eliminate from consideration all the openings which start with 1 P—K4 or 1 P—QB4 or (for the most part) 1 N—KB3. *Thus the area of required study is cut down enormously from the very start.*

1 P—Q4 is also irreproachable on theoretical grounds: the Pawn at Q4 commands the all-important center square K5, and in addition lines of development are opened for White's Queen and Queen Bishop.

In the vast majority of cases, Black will answer 1 P—Q4 with 1 . . . P—Q4. The merits of Black's reply are the same as those of White's first move: Black is enabled to control the important center square K5 and he opens lines for *his* Queen and Queen Bishop.

Come what may after these opening moves, each player has the consolation of knowing that he has adequate control of the center and cannot be smothered abjectly in the way the losers succumb in Part IV.

We are now ready to study the Stonewall pattern, *which gives White an aggressive development with splendid attacking possibilities.* White almost always has a marked initiative, and in the vast majority of cases obtains a long-lasting initiative. Instances in which White finds himself on the defensive are very hard to come by!

CHAPTER 2

STONEWALL ATTACK

I

Demolition Sacrifice at KR7

IN THIS notable example of the Stonewall Attack, White sets up the desired pattern in impeccable form. Without depending upon any serious blunders on Black's part, the game develops into a smashing attack against Black's castled King.

Note how White's most important offensive pieces play their characteristic roles: his *King Bishop* at Q3 points menacingly at Black's King-side; his *King Knight* is established formidably at K5, monopolizing the center; his *Queen* aims at KR5, striking at vulnerable points in Black's castled position; finally, the *King Rook* (after castling) executes the typical attacking maneuver R—KB3—KR3.

The terms in which White's play is described, speak for themselves: *smashing, attack, menacingly, formidably, monopolizing, striking, attacking*. All this is enough to give Black's King a persecution complex!

STONEWALL ATTACK

NEW YORK, 1950

WHITE	BLACK
E. Horowitz	*Amateur*
1 P—Q4	P—Q4

For an evaluation of these moves, see page 5 in the previous chapter.

2 P—K3	. . . .

Strictly speaking, White makes the text move because he is trying to steer the play into the Pawn pattern which he has observed, and with which you will become familiar. The advantages of this Pawn pattern will be discussed as the game progresses.

There are, of course, other good moves for White at this point. Until, however, you are ready to meet other defenses, with all their implied ramifications, you will find it useful to master one specific pattern.

DIAGRAM 1

(after 2 P—K3)
White intends to develop his
King Bishop to Q3.

From a theoretical point of view, White's last move has certain advantages and certain disadvantages. But, as you will see, the advantages outweigh the disadvantages.

Thus, White is now able to develop his King Bishop. This is a factor of the greatest importance, as the Bishop will play a big role in White's coming attacking plans.

True, 2 P—K3 blocks the development of White's Queen Bishop; but this piece is destined to have only minor scope in any event. Hence this disadvantage is of minor significance.

Incidentally, in reaching the desired Pawn pattern, it is essential for White to play his moves in the proper sequence, as indicated in this game.

(We return now to the position of Diagram 1.)

2 . . . .   N—KB3

This is an excellent developing move which has the merit of controlling K5 and also preparing for castling.

For the alternative developing move 2 . . . B—B4, which also controls K5 but leads to a totally different pattern, see page 45.

3 B—Q3   . . . .

This is one of the key moves in White's development. The Bishop move prepares for castling, sets the Bishop up on a strong attacking diagonal aiming at Black's prospective castled position, and disputes control of K4. As we shall see after White's next move, it is of the utmost importance for him to have the square K4 in his power.

3 . . . .   P—K3

Black follows suit, preparing for the development of his King Bishop.

4 N—Q2 !   . . . .

White intends to play P—KB4, one of the characteristic moves of his Pawn pattern. Once he has played that move, Black can bring his Knight to K5 without incurring any danger of having it driven away by P—KB3. (*See Diagram 2.*)

Hence, before playing P—KB4, White first plays out his Queen Knight to prevent . . . N—K5.

4 . . . .   P—B4

A good move theoretically, as it engages White's Queen Pawn and thus minimizes somewhat White's pressure on K5.

Of course White would not dream of replying 5 PxP ? as that would relax his grip on the valuable square K5. *Control of the center is of paramount importance.*

DIAGRAM 2

(after 4 N—Q2 *!*)
White has prevented . . .
N—K5 for good.

After the text there is a threat of . . . P—B5, driving
White's Bishop off the powerful attacking diagonal.

5 P—QB3 . . . .

Another characteristic move in the Stonewall pattern. White
supports the Queen Pawn and also creates a retreat for the
Bishop along the powerful attacking diagonal in the event that
it is menaced by . . . P—B5.

5 . . . . N—B3

Another useful developing move. Black threatens, if per-
mitted, to play . . . P—K4 with complete freedom and the
initiative to boot.

In this game we encounter a sharp tempo in the struggle for
control of the center. Where Black develops systematically,
there is a tense fight for control of the center from the very
beginning.

It is too early as yet for White to develop his basic plan of
the game, yet his play is by no means planless. The fight for
control of the center must necessarily absorb his thoughts. One
negligent move can yield the initiative to Black, as we see.

In the event of 5 . . . P—B5, trying to drive White's Bishop off the aggressive diagonal, White does not oblige by reacting passively with 6 B—K2, when the Bishop is left without attacking prospects. Instead, White plays 6 B—B2 *!* so that his Bishop exerts precisely the same aggressive effect as from Q3.

DIAGRAM 3

(after 5 . . . N—B3)
Black threatens to seize the
initiative by . . . P—K4.

6   P—KB4 *!*   . . . .

This move completes the Stonewall Pawn pattern. . . . P—K4 is permanently prevented, and White prepares to anchor his King Knight at the powerful outpost K5. Here the Knight will exert commanding influence on the enemy's terrain.

6 . . . .   **B—K2**

Black continues his development and prepares for castling. 6 . . . B—Q3 is pointless from the aspect of giving Black any attacking chances. With White's King Bishop Pawn at KB4, Black's "attacking" diagonal is blocked and the chances of attack are consequently nil.

Now we begin to see how the Stonewall pattern got its name!

7   KN—B3   . . . .

This Knight is headed for the formidable outpost K5.

7 . . . .   **Castles**

Black gets his King into safety—so he hopes—and looks forward to completing his development.

8   N—K5   . . . .

DIAGRAM 4

(after 8 N—K5)
White has established a
Knight very powerfully at K5.

White has now achieved his opening objectives: he has set up the Stonewall Pawn pattern, which gives him a firm grip on the center; he has posted his King Bishop at Q3 with strong attacking prospects; he has brought his King Knight to K5, emphasizing his grip on the center and his aggressive intentions towards Black's King.

8 . . . .   **Q—B2**

Black intends to "fianchetto" his Queen Bishop (. . . P—QN3 followed by . . . B—N2). Before he can do this, however, he must give his Queen Knight additional protection; hence . . . Q—B2.

Once Black's Queen Bishop is developed, he can start thinking of finding the most favorable squares for the placement of his Rooks.

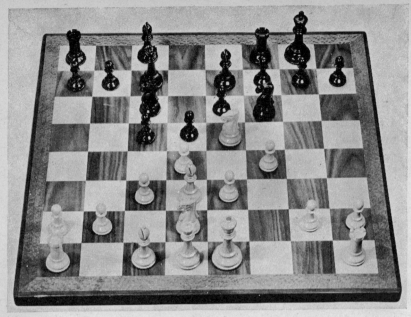

Figure 1

White has established his Knight firmly at K5—the key to his aggressive intentions in the STONEWALL ATTACK.

We can now ask ourselves: What is White's plan for the middle game? This requires a careful appraisal of the position.

Material is even. In development, Black seems to have a slight advantage; he has castled, moved his Queen and is on the point of developing his Queen Bishop. White lags in all the corresponding details, but they can easily be made up in short order.

Appraisal of the position shows that White has appreciably better prospects. Why?

Whereas Black has not posted one man beyond his fourth rank, White's King Knight is formidably placed at K5, well supported by two Pawns. This factor alone is enough to outweigh any item which is momentarily in Black's favor.

DIAGRAM 5

(after 8 . . . Q—B2)
White has aggressive intentions.

But there is another point: White's Bishop at Q3 aims
directly at Black's castled position. Nor can Black block the
attacking diagonal by . . . N—K5.

White's basic plan, then, is to aim for attack.

(*We return now to the position of Diagram 5.*)

9   Castles   . . . .

While automatically removing his King to safety, White enhances the force of the coming attack by bringing his King
Rook into action. (The possibility of R—B3—R3 has now been
created.)

White has shown good sense in adding the King Rook to his
attacking forces before embarking on an offensive. With his
Queen Bishop lacking possibilities of development for some
time, his Queen Rook is bound to be out of the game as well.
Hence White does well to make use of every attacking unit
available; a premature attack might well be disastrous.

Here we see *the value of planning*. Were he playing without
plan, failing to take every germane factor into consideration,
White might easily miss the significance of adding the King
Rook to his attacking forces. But since White is planning the
future with foresighted realization of what the attack requires,

DIAGRAM 6

(after 9 Castles)
White's attacking prospects
have been reinforced by the
possibility R—B3—R3.

his plan guides him toward the necessary steps for strengthening his attack.

(*We return now to the position of Diagram 6.*)

9 . . . . 　　　　　P—QN3

Black has several alternatives, none of them satisfactory.

Thus, he might play 9 . . . PxP, answered by 10 KPxP opening the diagonal for White's Queen Bishop, which can then move as soon as the Queen Knight clears the diagonal. Another point in White's favor is the opening of the King file for his Rooks. As 9 . . . PxP offers Black no compensating advantage, the move must be dismissed.

Secondly, Black might try 9 . . . P—B5. As has been pointed out, this does not drive the White Bishop off the attacking diagonal, as he has 10 B—B2 in reserve. Aside from this, 9 . . . P—B5 is bad on theoretical grounds. When one player (here White) has a powerful grip on the center, he welcomes situations in which Pawn captures in the center have become impossible; for in that case enemy diversions in the center are ruled out. Contrariwise, the player whose control of the center is weaker (here Black), should try to preserve the tension in the center in the hope of creating a diversion at some point. Hence 9 . . . PxP and 9 . . . P—B5 are theoretically unsatisfactory for Black.

Finally, there is the question of whether it pays Black to exchange Knights by 9 . . . NxN. At first sight this looks attractive, as it rids Black of a piece which is bound to be a thorn in his side. But the answer is still in the negative.

After 9 . . . NxN White recaptures 10 BPxN, with the result that the King Bishop file is opened for White. The power of White's Rook on KB1 is enhanced a millionfold; and we shall see in the games Alekhine-Prat and Morphy-Lewis (Part IV) how menacing a weapon the open King Bishop file can be.

An equally convincing argument against 9 . . . NxN is that after 10 BPxN Black's valuable protective Knight is driven away from KB3. The result is that the attack of White's King Bishop against KR7 (Black's KR2) becomes more virulent than ever, and it can be reinforced by such moves as Q—R5 and R—B3—R3. (The following game—Kujoth-Crittenden—gives you a good idea of the consequences of . . . NxN and White's recapture with his King Bishop Pawn.)

10 P—KN4   . . . .

DIAGRAM 7

(after 10 P—KN4)
White will drive away Black's valuable defensive Knight now at KB3.

White's violent thrust of the King Knight Pawn is made with several objectives in mind.

His basic idea is of course to drive away Black's King Knight from its present key defensive post, thereby intensifying the attack against KR7 by making available such moves as Q—R5.

Another point to P—KN4 is that after the Pawn advances to KN5, there are often opportunities to exchange it. *Pawn exchanges result in open lines.* In this case, the exchange of the Pawn would give White a new line for attack: the open King Knight file.

(*We return now to the position of Diagram 7.*)

10 . . . .   B—N2

DIAGRAM 8

(after 10 . . . B—N2)
Black "threatens" . . . NxN.
Why?

Now Black actually threatens to play 11 . . . NxN. But isn't this odd? A moment ago we said that 9 . . . NxN was bad. Now the claim is made that 11 . . . NxN would be good. What has happened to change the picture?

The point is this: After 11 . . . NxN; 12 BPxN Black would be able (after 10 . . . B—N2) to play 12 . . . N—K5 ! establishing and maintaining an outpost of his own. White's attacking plans would be permanently disrupted, as the attacking diagonal of his Bishop at Q3 would be neutralized.

It is interesting to dwell on this possibility. Note that *Black's hope of killing the attack is contingent on getting the upper hand in the center* (12 . . . N—K5); and this in turn is the result of 10 . . . B—N2, *a move which exerts pressure on the center.* And so, in the last analysis, it is the struggle for control of the center which determines the success or failure of the attack!

(*We return now to the position of Diagram 8.*)

11   Q—B3 *!*   . . . .

DIAGRAM 9

(after 11 Q—B3 *!*)
White has foiled Black's plan.
How?

Now Black's threat of . . . NxN fades into oblivion, as White's Queen move has reestablished his control of the center and has consequently assured the continued progress of his attack.

Thus, if 11 . . . NxN; 12 BPxN, N—K5 *?*; 13 NxN, PxN; 14 BxP and Black has lost a valuable Pawn without compensation.

(*We return now to the position of Diagram 9.*)

11 . . . .   P—QR3

A strange-looking move; how does it enhance Black's prospects? Is Black marking time? Is he waiting to see how White's plan unfolds?

DIAGRAM 10

(after 11 . . . P—QR3)
White attacks the King; Black
attacks . . . what?

Here is the reasoning behind Black's last move: The King-side is about as well-defended as it can be, and a regrouping of his forces would not improve his defensive prospects. Black therefore plans a Queen-side demonstration. He will advance his Queen-side Pawns in the hope of opening a file in that sector and in that way diverting White's attention from the King-side.

From a purely theoretical view, by the way, this plan is not very promising. For on the King-side White *attacks the King;* on the Queen-side Black *pursues a purely positional objective, which cannot harm White's King.* In fact, White's attentions now become so pressing that Black never gets any farther with his intended demonstration.

(*We return now to the position of Diagram 10.*)

12   P—N5   . . . .

Driving off the Knight.

12 . . . .   N—K1

After 12 . . . N—Q2 the game would take a similar course.

DIAGRAM 11

(after 12 . . . N—K1)
White decides to unleash a
violent attack.

White can now continue with 13 Q—R5 or 13 Q—R3 threatening mate and thereby provoking a weakening Pawn advance in front of the Black King. In the long run, this would probably result in a winning position for White. But, as it happens, White has a forceful way of penetrating immediately and smashing up the position of Black's King.

13   BxP *ch !*   . . . .

This sacrifice is the logical outcome of the Bishop's menacing position on the diagonal. Black's castled position now becomes so vulnerable that his King is exposed to a mating attack. (*See Diagram 12.*)

13   . . . .   KxB

13 . . . K—R1 is even worse, because of 14 Q—R5 threatening 15 B—N6 dis *ch* and 15 Q—R7 mate.

14   Q—R5 *ch*   K—N1
15   R—B3   . . . .

DIAGRAM 12

(after 13 BxP *ch!*)
White begins the demolition
of Black's castled position.

DIAGRAM 13

(after 15 R—B3)
White's King Rook swings
into action.

Note how White's forces are taking up the posts envisaged
in his original attacking plan. Now his idea is 16 R—R3 threatening 17 Q—R7 mate or 17 Q—R8 mate.

(*We return now to the position of Diagram 13.*)

> 15 . . . .   P—N3

This still offers some fight, whereas after 15 . . . P—B3;
16 P—N6 *!* mate follows at once.

> 16 Q—R6   . . . .

Still threatening R—R3 followed by Q—R7 mate or Q—R8 mate.

            16 . . . .   N—N2

Valiantly trying to shield his King.

            17 R—R3   N—KR4

DIAGRAM 14

(after 17 . . . N—KR4)
Black has barricaded the King
Rook file.

Now Black's plan has become clear. His Knight blocks the all-important King Rook file, preventing the execution of White's mating threat. White is a piece behind—he cannot afford to let up now. Another sacrifice is called for!

(*We return now to the position of Diagram 14.*)

            18 NxNP !   . . . .

Breaking Black's position wide open. The availability of the Knight for this sacrifice is a tribute to the power of this piece on the dominating square K5. (*See Diagram 15.*)

The threat is 19 Q—R8 mate. Black is left no choice.

            18 . . . .   PxN
            19 QxP *ch*   . . . .

DIAGRAM 15

(after 18 NxNP *!*)
White smashes the barricade!

Unhinging the support of Black's Knight at KR4. Black must interpose, for if 19 . . . K—R1 ?; 20 RxN mate.

19 . . . .   N—N2

Now White is two pieces down. How is he to continue the attack?

DIAGRAM 16

(after 19 . . . N—N2)
White can now win by a beautiful sacrifice!

20   R—R7 *? !*   . . . .

Overlooking 20 R—R8 *ch !!*, KxR; 21 Q—R6 *ch*, K—N1; 22 P—N6 ! when mate is unavoidable!

20 . . . .   B—Q3

This permits the Black Queen to guard the mate along the second rank. If instead 20 . . . R—B2; 21 Q—R6 is decisive because of the unanswerable threat of 22 R—R8 mate.

21   Q—R6   . . . .

DIAGRAM 17

(after 21 Q—R6)
White has a nasty threat.

With Black's King-side position perforated, White has no trouble thinking up new ways of keeping Black's King miserable. White intends 22 P—N6 followed by 23 R—R8 mate.

Of course, Black cannot escape by means of 21 . . . K—B2 for then 22 RxN *ch* wins his Queen. But he manages to find a desperate resource.

(*We return now to the position of Diagram 17.*)

21   . . . .   BxP

Pinning * White's King Knight Pawn and thus preventing P—N6—at least for the moment. (The reply 22 P—N6 *?* *?* *?* allows 22 . . . BxQ.)

22   PxB?   . . . .

* For the pin, see *Winning Chess*, p. 7.

Now the threat of P—N6 has to be met again. 22 R—R8 *ch*, K—B2; 23 Q—B6 *ch* is faster.

22	. . . .	RxP
23	P—N6	. . . .

DIAGRAM 18

(after 23 P—N6)
White threatens mate on the
move!

Black cannot escape unscathed by 23 . . . K—B1. There would follow: 24 R—R8 *ch*, K—K2; 25 QxN *ch*, K—Q3; 26 N—B4 *ch !* *, PxN; 27 BxR *ch* and it is all over.

(*We return now to the position of Diagram 18.*)

23	. . . .	R—N5 *ch*
24	K—R1	. . . .

24 K—B1 *?* is a mistake for then 24 . . . Q—B5 *ch* forces the exchange of Queens with a resulting easing of the tension for Black. As he is still a piece ahead, the exchange of Queens would win for him. (*See Diagram 19.*)

24	. . . .	RxNP

Black returns the rest of his booty—reluctantly, but what choice has he? If 24 . . . K—B1 (to guard against the mate); 25 N—B3 with threats of B—N5 or N—N5—not to mention

* Double attack. See *Winning Chess*, p. 50.

R—R8 *ch* followed by QxN *ch,* which White is holding in reserve.

DIAGRAM 19

(after 24 K—R1)
Black is still confronted with
a mating threat.

You must bear in mind that in actual practice it is extremely depressing to have the kind of position with which Black is burdened here: he is constantly on the defensive, his King has no secure refuge, new threats turn up at every move. For most players, the defensive is a thankless role indeed.

25   QxR   . . . .

White is now the exchange ahead and his pressure remains unabated. In one sense, it is even stronger than before, now that White's Bishop is ready to take a hand in the proceedings.

25   . . . .   R—KB1

To prevent 26 N—B3. If instead 25 . . . Q—B2 *P*; 26 R—R8 *ch !* * (*See Diagram 20.*)

26   N—B3 *!*   . . . .

There are other winning methods, but this is certainly the most pleasing.

* The overworked piece. See *Winning Chess,* p. 89.

DIAGRAM 20

(after 25 . . . R—KB1)
White has still another sacrifice up his sleeve!

26 . . . .   RxN
27 B—R6   . . . .

Setting up a murderous pin.* He threatens mate beginning
with 28 RxN *ch*.

27 . . . .   R—B2

The only defense. But now White strengthens the pin.

28 R—KN1   Resigns

DIAGRAM 21

(after 28 R—KN1)
Why does Black resign?

* For the pin, see *Winning Chess*, p. 7.

Black's capitulation is in order.

White's threat is 29 BxN followed by a discovered check *
with the Bishop which leads to mate.

If Black tries 28 . . . K—B1 White winds up convincingly
with 29 BxN *ch*, K—K2; 30 B—B6 *ch* or 29 . . . K—K1; 30
R—R8 *ch*, K—K2; 31 B—B8 *ch !*, K—K1 (if 31 . . . RxB; 32
R—R7 *ch*, K—Q1; 33 RxQ, KxR; 34 Q—N7 *ch* winning the
Rook in addition to the Queen); 32 B—Q6 dis *ch* winning the
Queen.

To summarize: White followed out his plan of attack consistently. He set up his pieces with a view to direct attack against
Black's King, particularly KR7. First driving away Black's guardian
King Knight, he concentrated his forces against the Black King,
sacrificing brilliantly in justifiable reliance on his ultimate success.

An interesting feature of the unfolding of White's attack is the
way his bottled-up Queen Bishop at last came to life and hammered
out the final decision against Black's harried King.

* For discovered check, see *Winning Chess*, p. 80.

CHAPTER 3

STONEWALL ATTACK

II

Normal Position for White

Y OU HAVE had an impressive demonstration of the power which can be unleashed by White in the Stonewall Attack.

The roles enacted by White's Pawns and pieces in Chapter 2 are fairly typical, and can therefore be reduced to formula. Hence you can familiarize yourself with the *typical, characteristic functions* of White's forces in the Stonewall Attack.

Of course, these functions are not purely mechanical. There is room for variety, as you will see in Chapter 4; there the Stonewall triumphs just as emphatically, but along somewhat different lines.

Remember also, that you must be the judge of timing. You are shown why this or that move is good; but *you* must be the judge of *when* it is good; when it is in order; when it can be played with maximum effect.

The White Pawns

The KING ROOK PAWN remains at KR2.*

The KING KNIGHT PAWN either remains at KN2 or else advances to KN4 and KN5 with the object of dislodging Black's useful defensive Knight from its post at KB3. This advance should not be undertaken until White has made considerable progress with his development.

* When we say that a Pawn remains at its original square, we mean merely that the over-all battle plan does not require a move by this Pawn. Later on in the game, there may be concrete and pressing reasons for moving the Pawn.

28

The KING BISHOP PAWN plays to KB4 where it assists White's Pawn at Q4 in keeping a strong grip on the center (K5) preventing . . . P—K4, and in many cases supporting a White Knight located on the magnificent outpost K5. Should Black capture White's powerful Knight at K5, the King Bishop Pawn recaptures at K5, opening the King Bishop file for White.

The KING PAWN plays to K3 early in the opening. In the event that Black plays . . . QBPxQP? White can recapture with his King Pawn, opening the King file for his Rooks and a diagonal for his Queen Bishop.

The QUEEN PAWN plays to Q4 on the first move, intending monopolistic control of K5 so that Black can never free himself by . . . P—K4. The Queen Pawn shares with the King Bishop Pawn the important function of supporting the powerful Knight outpost at K5.

The QUEEN BISHOP PAWN goes to QB3 where (like the King Pawn at K3) it supports the Queen Pawn as part of the typical Stonewall formation. Also, with this Pawn at QB3, the King Bishop at Q3 (if attacked by . . . P—QB5) can retreat to QB2 thus remaining on its powerful attacking diagonal.

The QUEEN KNIGHT PAWN remains at QN2.

The QUEEN ROOK PAWN remains at QR2.

The White Pieces

The KING KNIGHT goes to KB3 and later on occupies the powerful post K5. Here the Knight has a dominating post in the center and is also usefully placed in the event that White mounts a King-side attack.

The QUEEN KNIGHT goes to Q2 rather early in the opening in order to help prevent . . . N—K5, which would set up a counter-Stonewall formation on Black's part and block the magnificent attacking diagonal of White's King Bishop at Q3.

The KING BISHOP goes to Q3 on the third move (after 1 P—Q4 and 2 P—K3). Thereby the Bishop takes up his best square and acquires a splendid attacking line which sweeps all the way to KR7 (Black's KR2). Once Black has castled, his King becomes the direct target of an attack in which the King Bishop is the chief element.

The QUEEN BISHOP is developed rather late in the game. It is blocked by the White Pawns on K3 and KB4. The development of this Bishop is also impeded by the Queen Knight at Q2. However, this need not be a cause for worry, as Black is even more handicapped in his development. White's formation is so powerful that the delayed development of this Bishop is a relatively minor matter in this opening.

The KING ROOK reaches KB1 via castling. As the King Bishop Pawn will have gone to KB4, the Rook can often be played to KB3 and then to KR3 with a terrific King-side attack. (The Rook at KR3 cooperates with White's Bishop at Q3 in a concentrated attack against KR7.) In some cases, the King Rook gets an open King Bishop file when the King Bishop Pawn captures on K5 in the event of an exchange on that square.

The QUEEN ROOK generally does not play much of a role in the attack. This becomes clear when you recall that it takes quite a while before White's Queen Bishop moves from QB1. If the Bishop cannot move, then the Queen Rook in turn cannot be developed. This drawback is not fatal. But you must keep in mind that at some point where there is perhaps a lull in your attacking activities, you can pause for a breathing spell and bring out the Queen Bishop and Queen Rook. In any event, you must not allow yourself to be discouraged by the thought of this late development; Black's development is also hampered in much the same way.

The QUEEN has a number of possibilities, as one would expect from an opening like this one in which White has several attacking lines at his disposal. The Queen can play to K2 or (in cases where Black's King Knight has been driven away from KB3) to KN4 or KR5, with brutally candid threats against the Black King. Or the Queen can play to KB3 (when

this is necessary to prevent . . . N—K5), followed perhaps by
P—KN4 or in some cases by Q—N3.

Review: Salient objectives for White
(*1*) "Stonewall" Pawn pattern prevents Black from freeing himself
by . . . P—K4.
(*2*) White's Bishop at Q3 takes up magnificent attacking diagonal
directed at Black's KR2.
(*3*) White's Queen Knight at Q2 helps Bishop at Q3 to secure
complete White control of K4.
(*4*) White's King Knight generally occupies powerful outpost at
K5.
(*5*) After castling, White's attack can be augmented by R—KB3—
KR3.

CHAPTER 4

STONEWALL ATTACK

III

Swooping Down on the Open King Bishop File

In Chapter 2 White scored a magnificent victory by means of direct attack on Black's castled position. One of the important factors in that smashing attack was the powerfully posted White Knight at K5.

The strength of this Knight at K5, and the uneasiness which its presence inspires in the Black camp, are *typical:* the Knight at K5 is a harbinger of attack. In the following game, then, Black reasons, let us dispose of the troublesome Knight, making the defense relatively simple.

Black's reasoning sounds plausible, but he omits an important point. *Pawn captures open up lines.* Specifically, White's King Bishop Pawn recaptures on K5 and opens up the King Bishop file with devastating effect.

STONEWALL ATTACK
MILWAUKEE, 1949

WHITE	BLACK
R. Kujoth	R. Crittenden
1 P—Q4	P—Q4
2 P—K3	N—KB3
3 B—Q3	P—K3
4 P—KB4	. . . .

White has already established his mastery of K5, and has

played three of the four Pawn moves needed to establish the Stonewall pattern.

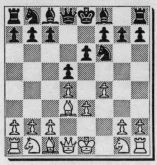

DIAGRAM 22

(after 4 P—KB4)
Why is 4 P—KB4 premature?

White's play has not been quite faultless. He has neglected to establish complete mastery of his K4. This could have been achieved by 4 N—Q2 (instead of 4 P—KB4). *Attaining the pattern is not enough; hair-sharp timing is also important.*

To exploit White's error, Black should play 4 . . . N—K5 *!* setting up a "counter-Stonewall" pattern.

(*We return now to the position of Diagram 22.*)

4 . . . .   QN—Q2 ?

This is wrong because Black misses his big opportunity (4 . . . N—K5 *!*).

Another drawback to the move is that it is unnecessarily conservative. The Knight should go to QB3 (after . . . P—QB4) where it exerts pressure on White's Queen Pawn. And it is obviously more aggressive to play a Knight to the third rank, where it has a better chance to come in contact with the enemy. When played to the second rank, the Knight has less chance to come in contact with the enemy, and Black's position takes on an excessively conservative, constricted appearance.

5 N—Q2   . . . .

Now White guards his K4 twice, so that . . . N—K5 is no longer feasible.

$$5 \quad . . . . \qquad\qquad \text{P—B4}$$
$$6 \quad \text{P—B3} \qquad\qquad . . . .$$

DIAGRAM 23

(after 6 P—B3)
White has set up the characteristic Stonewall pattern.

White has completed the Stonewall Pawn pattern. He has thorough control of K5 for setting up an outpost there (eventual N—K5); and he also has adequate control of K4 for preventing Black from setting up an outpost on that square.

$$6 \quad . . . . \qquad\qquad \text{PxP }?$$

This is a serious inaccuracy. The pressure on White's center is eliminated. White's already formidable center becomes even more stable, and cannot be upset by any future diversion on Black's part.

At this early stage, Black has made two wrong moves (4 . . . QN—Q2 ? and 6 . . . PxP ?) which have made things a lot easier for White. He now *knows* that Black's position will have a passive character, so that White is justified in evolving a policy of forthright aggression.

$$7 \quad \text{KPxP} \qquad\qquad . . . .$$

To retake with the Bishop Pawn would be faulty. The text opens up the diagonal for White's Queen Bishop, which is now certain of entering the fray at a much earlier stage than is customary in the Stonewall Attack. This consideration is another argument against 6 . . . PxP ?

DIAGRAM 24

(after 7 KPxP)
The exchange of center
Pawns has favored White.

The Stonewall formation always leads to a forceful initiative for White, even when the participation of his Queen Bishop is delayed. Now that White's Queen Bishop can become active more rapidly than usual, the indications are that White will build up an overwhelming position in short order.

7 . . . .   B—K2

7 . . . B—Q3 creates more problems for White, but they are problems that can be solved.

The question would be, how should White protect his King Bishop Pawn?

The most obvious method is 8 P—KN3, but this has the possible flaw that a later R—B3—R3 (after White castles) will have to be deferred until P—KN4 is played.

The other method of guarding the King Bishop Pawn is 8 QN—B3, intending N—K5 and enabling the Queen Bishop to protect the menaced Pawn.

Less good is 8 P—B5 ? (relaxing his grip on K5) because of
8 . . . P—K4 ! and Black immediately frees himself. Thus we
see how a silent but vital struggle for control of the center is
continually in progress.

        8   KN—B3   . . . .

Heading for K5, as per plan.

        8   . . . .   P—QN3

In order to develop his Queen Bishop.

        9   N—K5   . . . .

DIAGRAM 25

(after 9 N—K5)
White monopolizes the center.

White has attained his opening goal: the Stonewall Pawn
pattern gives him a stranglehold on the center, and his Knight
is firmly entrenched on the key square K5.

        9   . . . .   NxN ?

As Black's position is lacking in promising alternatives, this
move can hardly be called a mistake. Nevertheless, this capture
is bound to lead to grave difficulties for Black because of the
resulting opening of the King Bishop file. White requires very
little time to work up a menacing attack.

        10   BPxN !   . . . .

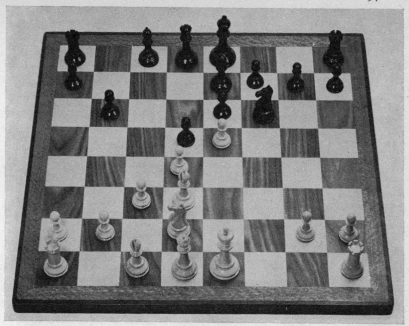

Figure 2

Whenever White's Knight at K5 is captured, it is vital to recapture
with the King Bishop Pawn. This greatly enhances White's initiative
in the STONEWALL ATTACK, as the opened King Bishop file becomes a powerful offensive weapon.

10 . . . .   N—Q2

The open King Bishop file is a powerful medium of attack.
This is generally the case where *Pawn captures have opened
up avenues of attack.*

Note that the Pawn capture on K5 has also opened up a line
of offense—a diagonal—for White's Queen Bishop. This piece
will soon display formidable qualities.

A final consequence is that Black's valuable King Knight has
been driven away from KB3, so that the Black King is deprived
of the services of his best protective unit—services that are
generally available as a matter of routine.

DIAGRAM 26

(after 10 . . . N—Q2)
White's open King Bishop file
is an avenue of attack.

11   Castles   . . . .

By castling (automatically getting his King into safety, by
the way) White immediately makes use of the open King
Bishop file: his King Rook immediately strikes along the whole
length of the open file.

DIAGRAM 27

(after 11 Castles)
White's King Rook is posted
for action on the open King
Bishop file.

White can now formulate his general plan of the game.

White's situation is ideal: his Bishop on Q3 points menacingly at Black's King-side; White's King Rook is poised for action on the King Bishop file; White's Queen has such powerful thrusts as Q—B3 or Q—N4 or Q—R5 in reserve.

Black's King-side is denuded of protection and the disproportion of attacking and defensive forces is even heightened by the fact that a single move by White's Knight will bring his Queen Bishop into action.

All indications are that White's tactical superiority will assure him quick victory.

(We return now to the position of Diagram 27.)

11 .... P—QR4

Black is afraid to castle right into the crossfire of White's attacking forces. It is therefore Black's hope that he can remove one of White's most formidable attacking units by exchange: Black intends 12 . . . B—R3. Black is operating on the familiar theory that the defender should always try to ease his difficulties by simplifying. Whether White will permit this simplification is something else again.

12 Q—N4 ....

DIAGRAM 28

(after 12 Q—N4)
How should Black parry the attack on his King Knight Pawn?

By threatening the deadly QxNP White leaves his opponent no time to carry out his simplifying idea. White, you observe, is developing his Queen without loss of time, as Black must spend a move to guard the menaced King Knight Pawn.

12 . . . .   P—N3

Ordinarily, castling is the simplest and most effective way to guard the Pawn—but not here, where the castled position lacks adequate defense. Thus after 12 . . . Castles White plays 13 Q—R5 threatening mate. (Note how effectively White's Queen and his King Bishop cooperate in making this threat possible.) Now Black can parry the threat only by weakening his castled position in some decisive manner. Here are the alternatives:

I. 13 . . . P—R3; 14 N—B3 threatening the crushing break-through sacrifice 15 BxP etc.

II. 13 . . . P—N3; 14 Q—R6 and Black is helpless against a wealth of threats, such as R—B3—R3 or N—B3—N5.

III. 13 . . . P—B4; 14 PxP e.p., NxP; 15 RxN !, RxR; 16 QxP ch, K—B1; 17 N—B3, RxN; 18 PxR and White retains his attack with a Pawn to the good.

13 B—B2 !   . . . .

Naturally White has no intention of indulging Black's eager-ness to simplify by . . . B—R3.

13 . . . .   B—N4

Black is desperate, realizing that if he castles, White simply plays 14 N—B3 with a field day against the enfeebled black squares (15 B—R6 etc.). (See Diagram 29.)

14 N—B4 !   . . . .

A clever discovered attack * which increases Black's diffi-culties.

* For discovered attack, see Winning Chess, p. 67.

DIAGRAM 29

(after 13 . . . B—N4)
White has a remarkable reply
at his disposal.

Thus, if 14 . . . BxB; 15 N—Q6 *ch*, K—B1; 16 RxP *ch* (note the power of the Rook along the open file!), K—N1; 17 BxP *!* and Black can resign. (If 17 . . . P—KR4; 18 B—R7 mate!)

14 . . . .   PxN

Black does not care to retreat 14 . . . B—K2; an instance of the reluctance of all chessplayers—masters as well as amateurs! —to admit their mistakes.

It is true that after 14 . . . B—K2 White can play 15 N—Q6 *ch*, BxN; 16 PxB with an easy victory because of his complete mastery of the black squares.

15 BxB   . . . .

Now White still monopolizes the black squares and in addition he has a devastating attack.

15 . . . .   Q—B2
16 RxP *!!*   . . . .

White's Rook sacrifice is brilliant indeed, but what is more important for the student is the realization that the brilliant sacrifice is made possible by White's crushing grip on the open file, and that this in turn was made possible by a *Pawn capture*.

DIAGRAM 30

(after 16 RxP *!!*)
White has sacrificed a Rook—
inspiration or perspiration?

16 . . . .   KxR
17 R—B1 *ch*   . . . .

DIAGRAM 31

(after 17 R—B1 *ch*)
White cashes in on the open
King Bishop file.

17 . . . .   K—N2

There is no satisfactory defense. Obviously 17 . . . K—K1
will not do because of 18 QxP mate.

Nor is 17   . . K—N1 any better: 18 QxP *ch*, K—N2; 19
Q—B7 mate.

17 . . . N—B3 requires greater exertion on White's part, but the result is the same: 18 RxN *ch,* K—N2; 19 B—R6 *ch ! !,* KxB; 20 RxP *ch !,* PxR; 21 QxNP mate.

Or 17 . . . N—B3; 18 RxN *ch,* K—K1; 19 B—R4 *ch* (a "smite" from the other direction!), B—Q2; 20 QxP *ch* etc. (Black's Bishop is pinned.[*])

> 18   B—R6 *ch ! !*   . . . .

Another beautiful sacrifice which enmeshes Black's King in a mating net from which he cannot escape.

> 18   . . . .   KxB

Of course, if 18 . . . K—N1; 19 QxKP mate.

> 19   R—B7   . . . .

Threatens 20 Q—R4 mate.

> 19   . . . .   Q—Q1

To defend the threat. But there is another threat!

DIAGRAM 32

(after 19 . . . Q—Q1)
White concludes with another
brilliant sacrifice!

> 20   RxP *ch ! !*   KxR
> 21   QxNP mate

* For the pin, see *Winning Chess,* p. 7.

Black is two Rooks and a Knight ahead, but he bites the dust just the same! Brilliant as this conclusion is, we must repeat that White's consistent execution of his attacking plan is even more impressive.

This attacking plan was based on the concentration of White's forces on the King-side, and the lack of defensive power in the same sector. It was Black's faulty exchange on move 9, followed by the opening of the King Bishop file, that allowed White to carry out his plan so rapidly and so impressively.

CHAPTER 5

QUEEN'S GAMBIT DECLINED

Black Evades the Stonewall Attack

In the previous two games we have had an unforgettable impression of the power of White's attack when he adopts the Stonewall formation.

It is quite natural, under the circumstances, for Black to cast about for other lines of play. If the Stonewall pattern gives him so much trouble, why not choose some other pattern? Why not draw the sting from White's attack?

Reasoning along these lines, Black strives for a different pattern. But his life is not a happy one.

QUEEN'S GAMBIT DECLINED
BUDAPEST, 1926

WHITE	BLACK
H. Kmoch	G. Nagy
1 P—Q4	P—Q4
2 P—K3	B—B4

With this saucy Bishop move, Black definitely announces that he has no intention of submitting to the kind of cramped position with which he is burdened in the Stonewall formation.

White can immediately forget about proceeding along Stonewall lines: it would be pointless to play B—Q3, as Black could simply play . . . BxB or . . . P—K3 with a comfortable game. All thoughts of attack on KR7 are out of the question. White must therefore seek a different approach.

DIAGRAM 33

(after 2 . . . B—B4)
The Stonewall formation is no
longer possible.

3   P—QB4 !   . . . .

This is the new approach. White opens up a diagonal for his
Queen (intention: Q—N3) in the hope of exploiting the ab-
sence of Black's Queen Bishop from the Queen-side.

As we shall see, the task of defending Black's Queen Knight
Pawn is far from easy.

3   . . . .   P—QB3

DIAGRAM 34

(after 3 . . . P—QB3)
Black's last move is an important part of his strategic plan.

Black has seen the danger and prepared for it. He means to answer Q—N3 with . . . Q—N3. Hence White bides his time, and continues his development. He foresees that Q—N3 will yet be effective.

4   N—KB3   N—B3
5   PxP   . . . .

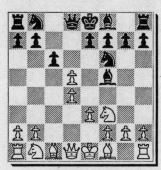

DIAGRAM 35

(after 5 PxP)
Black has a problem: how shall he recapture?

Now Black has a problem which often turns up in this book: how should he recapture in order to retain control of the center? If he retakes with a piece, then sooner or later White will be able to advance P—K4 with monopoly of the center.

Thus Black concludes that the only sound method of recapture is with the Pawn. (This, by the way, is one of the reasons for 3 . . . P—QB3.)

5   . . . .   PxP

Now that Black retains his firm foothold in the center, he need not fear any central expansion on White's part by way of P—K4.

6   N—B3   P—K3

The normal developing move 6 . . . N—B3 is strongly answered by 7 Q—N3 *!* attacking the Queen Knight Pawn. If then 7 . . . Q—N3; 8 B—N5 and Black encounters the same kind of difficulties as in the text continuation.

7   N—K5 *!*   . . . .

DIAGRAM 36

(after 7 N—K5 *!*)
Again White has a powerful
Knight at K5!

As in the Stonewall Variation proper, the posting of White's King Knight on the valuable central square K5 is very strong.

Now that Black has played . . . P—K3 (necessary for the development of his King Bishop), his Queen Bishop can no longer return to QB1. White has two moves in reserve which will be troublesome to meet: B—N5 *ch* and/or Q—N3. He also has other threats.

7   . . . .   B—Q3

After the plausible developing move 7 . . . QN—Q2 *P* Black finds himself in serious trouble. White plays 8 P—KN4 *!* proving to Black that the confident development . . . B—KB4 has its thorny aspects.

After 7 . . . QN—Q2 *P*; 8 P—KN4 *!* Black must not play 8 . . . NxN *P* because of 9 PxN winning at least a piece. Thus, if

Figure 3

Whenever Black develops his Bishop to KB4 in the QUEEN'S GAMBIT DECLINED, he must always reckon with a possible resulting weakness of his Queen Knight Pawn. This is best exploited by White's Q—N3. (This position arises after 8 Q—N3.)

9 . . . BxP; 10 Q—R4 *ch*, N—Q2; 11 QxB. Or if 9 . . . NxP; 10 Q—R4 *ch*, K—K2 (if 10 . . . Q—Q2; 11 B—N5 winning the Queen *); 11 Q—N4 *ch*, and wins: on 11 . . . K—K1; 12 B—N5 *ch* wins the Queen, and on 11 . . . K—Q2; 12 QxP *ch* wins the Queen Rook, as 12 . . . K—K1; 13 B—N5 *ch* leads to mate.

On the other hand, if 7 . . . QN—Q2 *?;* 8 P—KN4 *!*, B—N3; 9 P—KR4 *!* (threatening to win the Bishop with P—R5), P—KR3; 10 NxB, PxN; 11 B—Q3, K—B2; 12 Q—B2 and White has an easy win because of Black's smashed-up King's position.

* The pin. See *Winning Chess*, p. 7.

This is our first indication that 2 . . . B—B4 can involve
Black in serious trouble.

$$8 \quad Q—N3 \, ! \qquad \ldots$$

Taking advantage of the fact that Black's Bishop at KB4 cannot retreat to QB1 to guard the Queen Knight Pawn.

$$8 \quad \ldots \qquad Q—N3$$
$$9 \quad B—N5 \, ch \qquad \ldots$$

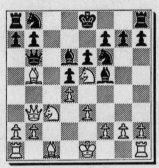

DIAGRAM 37

(after 9 B—N5 *ch*)
White increases the pressure
without any loss of time.

$$9 \quad \ldots \qquad KN—Q2$$

After 9 . . . N—B3? Black loses a Pawn by 10 BxN *ch*,
PxB; 11 QxQ, PxQ; 12 NxQBP.

However, after his last move Black threatens to slip out
deftly by 10 . . . BxN; 11 PxB, Castles. Hence White must
find some way of maintaining the pressure.

$$10 \quad NxN \, ! \qquad NxN$$

Black's position is very difficult, one of the chief reasons for
this being that his Bishop at KB4 plays no role in the proceedings.

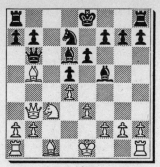

DIAGRAM 38

(after 10 . . . NxN)
Who will gain control of the
open Queen Bishop file?

11 B—Q2 !   . . . .

The right way to maintain the pressure is to clear the open
Queen Bishop file for occupation by White's Queen Rook.

Black cannot play 11 . . . Castles (K), losing his Knight.

Nor can he play 11 . . . Castles (Q), because of 12 QR—B1
(threatens to win the Queen), K—N1 (getting out of the discovered check); 13 N—R4 and wins.

Trying to get rid of the pin is also fatal: 11 . . . P—QR3 *?*;
12 BxN *ch* winning the Queen! *

What other possibility remains? If Black tries 11 . . . R—Q1
(in order to guard the pinned Knight and make castling possible), then White gets a tremendous game with 12 N—R4, Q—
B2; 13 QR—B1, Q—N1; 14 N—B5 etc. Here again Black's
Bishop at KB4 remains idle.

11 . . . .   QR—B1

Black tries to neutralize the pressure on the open file. The
loss of castling after 12 BxN *ch*, KxB does not bother him, as
his King would be reasonably safe and most of the uncomfortable pressure would be dissipated.

* Discovered attack. See *Winning Chess,* p. 67.

12   Castles (K)   B—N1

Planning a cumbersome method of accomplishing castling. His intention is 12 . . . Castles; 13 BxN, Q—Q3 threatening checkmate and thereby winning White's exposed Bishop and reestablishing material equality.*

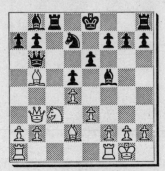

DIAGRAM 39

(after 12 . . . B—N1)
Why is P—B4 indicated as
White's next move?

13   P—B4   . . . .

Blocking the mate threat and thereby preventing Black from castling.

13   . . . .   Q—Q3

He protects his Knight in order to be able to castle. Note that even now 13 . . . P—QR3 ? would lose the Queen (14 BxN *ch* etc.).

14   QR—B1 !   Castles
15   N—R4 !   . . . .

With the murderous threat of 16 B—N4. And Black's Bishop at KB4 is still an innocent bystander!

* Double attacks. See *Winning Chess*, p. 50.

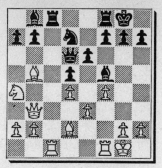

DIAGRAM 40

(after 15 N—R4!)
Black's Queen is in serious
danger.

15 . . . .   Q—K2

This is about the only move at Black's disposal; but now he
loses a Pawn by force.

16	B—N4	B—Q3
17	BxB	QxB
18	BxN	QxB
19	N—B5	Q—B3
20	QxNP	QxQ
21	NxQ	. . . .

DIAGRAM 41

(after 21 NxQ)
Black's game is hopeless.

White is a Pawn ahead and has an easily won game. In his concern about the positional threat of N—Q6, which would weaken his Pawn structure, Black blunders badly:

| 21 | . . . . | KR—Q1 ? |
| 22 | NxR | Resigns |

The important lesson this game teaches is that Black's avoidance of the Stonewall pattern by 2 . . . B—B4 is not an unmixed blessing. True, he prevents White from establishing the desired attacking formation; yet the posting of the Queen Bishop at KB4 exposes this piece to attack and leaves Black's Queen-side in a vulnerable state.

At this point we conclude our study of the Stonewall Attack as the recommended opening for you to adopt when playing the White pieces.

We turn now to the problems of playing the Black pieces and finding satisfactory replies to 1 P—K4 and 1 P—Q4.

From the three previous games we have seen how White conducts the middle game that evolves from the Stonewall pattern.

♛ PART TWO ♛

Playing With the Black Pieces
Against 1 P—K4

CHAPTER 6

What Defense Shall I Play
Against 1 P—K4 . . . ?

I F, AS we have seen, it is difficult to choose an opening line with White, the difficulty seems enhanced when you have the Black pieces. For when your opponent has the first move, *you are dependent on him* for the initial decision: will he advance the King Pawn or the Queen Pawn?

In this section, we assume that your opponent begins with 1 P—K4. Then, if you reply 1 . . . P—K4, you are again confronted with the nightmare of thousands of possible variations. Will he choose the Ruy Lopez, or the Giuoco Piano, or the Four Knights' Game, or the Evans Gambit, or the Danish Gambit, or the innumerable variants of the King's Gambit?

Your anxiety about these Unknowns is enough to put you in a frame of mind which is far from conducive to playing the best chess of which you are capable. Worse yet, when you cannot foresee what opening will be played, you cannot plan the game along lines which are familiar and favorable to you.

Let us see if we can apply some sharp and conclusive thinking to this problem. If you reply 1 . . . P—K4, you are exposed, as we have seen, to a terrifyingly large number of possible openings. The logical decision, then, is to play one of the so-called "irregular" defenses. *By ruling out 1 . . . P—K4, we also rule out all the variations which result from that move.*

This drastic elimination has two valuable features: (1) it rules out a huge number of variations, which need no longer be studied—or feared; (2) it enables you to play on familiar terrain—to get the kind of middle game you want, to make use of leading ideas and basic concepts which you will have studied and digested previously.

The defense which we recommend for this purpose has the three qualities previously listed as indispensable for an opening which yields good middle game prospects: (1) it assures Black a logical and systematic development which will give his pieces ample scope in the middle game; (2) it begins a stern fight for control of the center from the very first move; (3) It is immune to changes in style, theory etc. because Black's characteristic pattern is based on sound strategical concepts.

The recommended line is called the Sicilian Defense: 1 . . . P—QB4. Before considering this defense, we need to correct a widespread misapprehension about the psychology of playing the Black pieces.

Most players feel at home with White, because they control, so they think, the choice of opening. Actually, *they control only the choice of the first move.* On the other hand, most players feel uncomfortable with the Black pieces, for reasons that are obvious. Yet once the first move has been made, Black has a very valuable choice—*one which is often a veto.*

When White plays 1 P—K4, he is generally expecting to play a specific opening that evolves after the "normal" reply 1 . . . P—K4. But here Black's veto comes into action: by playing a defense of his choice, *he* dictates the opening, and consequently the kind of subsequent play, that will result from his first move.

Here, then, we have one great merit of the Sicilian Defense: by playing 1 . . . P—QB4, Black announces *his* terms for the coming struggle, steers the game into the kind of channels he wants it to follow. And here another advantage of the Sicilian Defense soon becomes apparent: since White's second move (2 N—KB3) is more or less standard, Black can actually select the particular variation he wants to play.

The form of the Sicilian which he wants is known as the

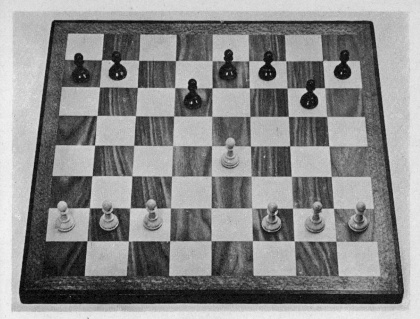

Figure 4

*This is the characteristic Pawn formation of the DRAGON VARIA-
TION. Note the powerful long diagonal for Black's King Bishop,
and also Black's open Queen Bishop file.*

Dragon Variation, possibly from the shape of Black's Pawn
formation (see Figure 4, shown above). Here are the opening
moves:

1	P—K4	P—QB4
2	N—KB3	N—QB3
3	P—Q4	PxP
4	NxP	N—B3

Black develops with a threat (. . . NxP). Note that he has
brought out two pieces in four moves—a very satisfactory rate
of development.

5	N—QB3	. . . .

White defends with a developing move. You will observe
that he does not have the kind of broad center that we see in
the last four games of this book: his Queen Pawn was removed
as soon as it reached Q4. Consequently Black is in no danger
of being overrun by an overwhelming White Pawn center; a
keen struggle for control of the center is already in progress,
and will continue to rage unabated.

5 . . . .   P—Q3

This prepares in due course for the development of Black's
Queen Bishop. Once this Bishop moves, Black will be able to
play his Queen Rook to QB1, where it will be functioning on a
half-open file, with White's Queen Bishop Pawn as a potential
target.

Even at this early stage you can see that the Sicilian is a
fighting defense: Black develops rapidly, he fights for the center, he creates possibilities for the aggressive functioning of his
forces later on. If White had any ideas about bang-bang attack,
he has had to relinquish them.

6 B—K2   P—KN3 !

DIAGRAM 42

(after 6 . . . P—KN3 !)
Black prepares to post his
King Bishop on the long diag-
onal.

This and the following Bishop development are the characteristic moves of the Dragon Variation.

7   Castles   B—N2

We have gone far enough to get acquainted with the basic ideas of the Dragon Variation.

The "fianchettoed" Bishop strikes along the diagonal to fight for control of the center, particularly the square Q5 (White's Q4). Black develops favorably and quickly. He cannot be driven back in the center. Later on he will operate on the half-open Queen Bishop file. As he has two center Pawns to White's one, he will often advance in the center to open up the position for more effective action by his pieces.

Altogether a very cheerful picture for the player of the Black pieces, and one which is borne out in actual practice. Black has good fighting chances and an opportunity to plan constructively. The basic strategic ideas, as revealed in the illustrative games, are easy to grasp and sharply defined. So let us turn to these games to see how the Dragon Variation fares against worthy opponents.

CHAPTER 7

DRAGON VARIATION

I

White Cannot Afford Indifferent Play

Oɴᴇ ᴏꜰ the most attractive features of the Dragon Variation is that White cannot get by with merely indifferent play. Planless moves on White's part merely result in a correspondingly promising middle game for Black.

The game which follows is a good instance. White plays carelessly; his center Pawns disappear; his development is slow; Black's "Dragon" Bishop holds sway over the long diagonal; an advantageous exchange gives Black two long-range Bishops.

All this adds up to a strong initiative for Black. The players change roles, and the defender (Black) becomes the attacker.

SICILIAN DEFENSE
POSTAL GAME, 1949

WHITE	BLACK
A. *Giusti*	M. *Nutrizio*
i P—K4	P—QB4

As we have seen, Black, by playing this move, avoids all the innumerable possibilities which stem from 1 . . . P—K4.

In that sense, the Sicilian may be said to be an *aggressive* defense on Black's part.

It is also aggressive in the sense that Black has certain ideas of his own which he wants to carry out: he is not merely waiting passively to see what White will do.

Before going on to our study of the Dragon Variation proper, we should note that the most popular reply to 1 . . . P—QB4 is 2 N—KB3, as in the sequence of moves which leads to the Dragon Variation.

The only alternative second move for White which is encountered fairly frequently is 2 N—QB3. This leads almost invariably to a complex maneuvering game along these lines: 2 . . . N—QB3; 3 P—KN3, P—KN3; 4 B—N2, B—N2; 5 P—Q3 and now Black has various methods, one of the best being 5 . . . P—K3; 6 B—K3, Q—R4; 7 N—K2, N—Q5; 8 Castles, N—K2.

As Black has quite a comfortable game with an easy development, this line is a favorite, for the most part, with masters who have made a thorough study of it—and is therefore rarely encountered in the games of amateurs.

2	N—KB3	N—QB3
3	P—Q4	. . . .

The advance of this Pawn is desirable and logical, as it opens up lines of development for White's forces.

DIAGRAM 43

(after 3 P—Q4)
What is Black's only good reply?

3 . . . .   PxP

This is the only move worth considering: White must not be allowed to continue P—Q5 driving back Black's Knight and getting one of those overwhelming central Pawn structures which, as we shall see in Part IV (Alekhine-Prat) stifle the opponent's later attempts to get a foothold in the center.

4	NxP	N—B3
5	N—QB3	P—Q3
6	B—K2	P—KN3
7	Castles	B—N2

The setup achieved here by Black can be considered the basic formation of the Dragon Variation. The chief characteristics are these:

Figure 5

This is "the normal position" of the DRAGON VARIATION. Even at this early stage, the power of the "Dragon" Bishop is felt on the long diagonal.

(1) the King Bishop is fianchettoed to strike along the long diagonal which has been opened up as a result of the Pawn exchange on move 3.

(2) Black's Queen Pawn goes to Q3 to give him a Pawn foothold in the center.

Note that Black's fianchettoed King Bishop hits at White's Q4 just as in the game Scheltinga-Grau (page 182) Black's fianchettoed Queen Bishop hits at White's K4. Any attempt to upset Black by P—K5 is well neutralized; and since Black is perfectly secure in the center, we may forecast a satisfactory development for him.

DIAGRAM 44

(after 7 . . . B—N2)
Black's fianchettoed "Dragon"
Bishop strikes along the long
diagonal.

At this very moment Black is threatening to win a Pawn by 8 . . . NxP ! If then 9 N(B3)xN, Black captures the Knight on White's Q4. Or if 9 N(Q4)xN, Black replies 9 . . . NxN and retains the Pawn advantage in the ensuing complications. This gives us some idea of the power of the fianchettoed Bishop.

(*We return now to the position of Diagram 44.*)

8   N—N3   . . . .

By withdrawing the menaced Knight from Q4, White parries the threat just described. Another way to meet the threat was

8 B—K3, protecting the threatened Knight with a developing move.

8	. . .	Castles
9	P—B4	. . . .

White proceeds aggressively in the center, but it would be more accurate to play the developing move 9 B—K3.

DIAGRAM 45

(after 9 P—B4)
Black has a surprising counter.

9	. . .	P—QN4!?

A strange-looking move which has points. For White to answer 10 NxP allowing 10 . . . NxP is hardly desirable—why give up a valuable center Pawn for a relatively unimportant wing Pawn?

10	BxP	. . . .

But this too is a feeble move, as it leads to the transaction just described.

Best was 10 B—B3 (guarding the King Pawn), P—N5; 11 N—Q5, NxN; 12 PxN, N—R4 leading to a game with equal chances.

10	. . .	NxP!
11	BxN	. . .

Or 11 NxN, Q—N3 *ch* (double attack *) winning the Bishop and reestablishing material equality.

DIAGRAM 46

(after 11 BxN)
Has Black blundered? !

White has won a piece and seems about to win a second one with the double attack on Knight and Rook. But Black has a way out:

11	....	Q—N3 *ch*
12	K—R1	QxB

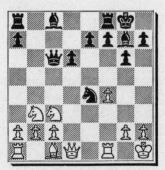

DIAGRAM 47

(after 12 . . . QxB)
Black has the advantage.

* For double attack, see *Winning Chess*, p. 50.

To formulate a strategical plan in this situation is very easy for Black. He has two center Pawns, White has none—hence Black will lord it over his opponent in the center. Black has two Bishops, both with fine scope; White's minor pieces are in-effectual (particularly his Knight on QN3) and he has trouble completing his development. Black has the open Queen Knight and Queen Bishop files for his Rooks. Of course the "Dragon" Bishop strikes powerfully along his diagonal. All these factors make it a simple matter for Black to find good moves.

If now 13 NxN, QxN; 14 R—K1, Q—N2; 15 P—B3, B—K3 with a perfect "Dragon" position for Black. Hence White tries another way.

(*We return now to the position of Diagram 47.*)

> ### 13   N—Q5   . . . .

Threatening to win the Queen by 14 NxP *ch*—an instance of double attack.

> ### 13   . . . .   R—K1

Guarding against White's threat. Note, by the way, that White is unable to develop his Bishop because he has to guard the Queen Knight Pawn, which is attacked by Black's fianchet-toed Bishop. This is a good example of the "Dragon" Bishop's powers.

> ### 14   P—B3   B—N2

Now the other Bishop is developed effectively (threat: . . . QxN). Black's Bishops have tremendous sway—and White's Bishop is not even developed!

Worse yet, as far as White is concerned, is that his Knight must retreat from Q5. But where?

If 15 N—N4 ? ? there follows 15 . . . N—N6 *ch !* (discov-ered attack *) followed by 16 . . . QxP mate! This gives us an idea of the power of Black's Bishop at QN2.

---

* For discovered attack, see *Winning Chess*, p. 67.

(We return now to the position of Diagram 48.)

DIAGRAM 48

(after 14 . . . B—N2)
Black's Bishops are functioning admirably.

15 N—K3 . . . .

This stops the potential mate at White's KN2, at the cost of postponing the development of his Bishop.

If given time, White hopes to play N—R5, getting rid of one of the troublesome Bishops.

15 . . . . P—QR4 *!*

Prevents N—R5. Black consistently cuts down the mobility of the White Knights.

16 N—Q4 Q—Q2
17 P—B5 . . . .

Trying desperately for some counterplay.

17 . . . . P—K4
18 N—K2 B—KR3 *!?*

Up to this point Black's play has been logical and strong, and he should now continue . . . P—Q4 with a view to . . . P—Q5. Black's position would then become overwhelming in short order.

DIAGRAM 49

(after 18 . . . B—KR3 *!?*)
Black has missed the most
precise line.

19	N—N4	B—N2
20	PxP	RPxP
21	N—R6 *ch ?*	. . . .

Falling into a diabolical trap.

| 21 | . . . . | BxN |
| 22 | BxB | . . . . |

White's position looks good for the first time, as the black
squares on Black's King-side have been weakened. But White
is hopelessly lost!

DIAGRAM 50

(after 22 BxB)
Black has a brilliant win!

| 22 | . . . . | Q—R6 *! ! !* |
| 23 | PxQ | . . . . |

If White moves the menaced Bishop, then 23 . . . N—
N6 *ch* leads to mate next move!

| 23 | . . . . | N—B7 *dbl ch* |
| 24 | K—N1 | NxP mate *!* |

In this game we see how Black can get a strong initiative against
inexact play by White. White's Knights made too many moves; his
Queen Bishop did not get out in time; he surrendered control of the
center. Black on the other hand developed his pieces favorably and
consistently and controlled the center, whereupon opportunities for
attack readily became available.

Black won the game with a clever trap, but his victory was not
accidental: his superior development made the win possible.

CHAPTER 8

DRAGON VARIATION

II

Normal Position for Black

IN CHAPTER 7 you saw how powerful Black's position in the Dragon Variation can become against inferior play. We purposely began with a weakly played game by White in order to approach the problems of this variation in the simplest manner.

That is to say, you had an opportunity to see how Black's pieces and Pawns are placed in the first ten moves or so. In the later games, beginning with Chapter 9, you will see how Black's forces perform against stronger play on White's part.

If you study the *characteristic* development and function of the Black pieces, as described in this chapter, you will be amply prepared to meet the stronger lines at White's disposal.

Again we stress the precautionary advice of Chapter 3: remember that you must be the judge of timing. You are shown why this or that move is good; but *you* must be the judge of *when* it is good; when it is in order; when it can be played with maximum effect.

The Black Pawns

The KING ROOK PAWN remains at KR2.

The KING KNIGHT PAWN plays to KN3 early in the opening to permit the fianchetto of the "Dragon" Bishop at KN2, the characteristic move of the whole variation.

The KING BISHOP PAWN remains at KB2.

The KING PAWN generally remains at K2, but on occasion it advances to K4. As this advance leaves the Queen Pawn backward on an open file, there will generally be good reason for . . . P—K4. As a rule, the move is tied up with a subsequent . . . P—Q4. Or, sometimes (as in Sköld-Lundin) . . . P—K4 makes it possible for Black to gain the square K4 for his pieces. In most cases, . . . P—K3 is to be avoided in this variation, as it results in Pawn weaknesses without compensating advantages.

The QUEEN PAWN plays to Q3 early in the opening. When a favorable opportunity arises, this Pawn advances to Q4 with a perceptible freeing of Black's game.

The QUEEN BISHOP PAWN disappears very early in the opening through the exchange . . . QBPxQP. Nevertheless, the expendable Queen Bishop Pawn renders a valuable service, for this exchange of Pawns makes it impossible for White to expand into a mighty Pawn center, and also creates a half-open Queen Bishop file for Black which can be very useful for his Queen Rook.

The QUEEN KNIGHT PAWN generally remains at QN2. In some lines (see Giusti-Nutrizio) it plays to QN4, even without the preliminary protective move . . . P—QR3.

The QUEEN ROOK PAWN has varied possibilities. Sometimes it remains on QR2; in other games it advances to QR3, occasionally to prepare for . . . P—QN4; and sometimes . . . P—QR4 is played, chiefly with a view to . . . P—R5 harrying a White Knight at QN3.

The Black Pieces

The KING KNIGHT plays to KB3 where it attacks White's King Pawn and keeps it under observation. Whenever White plays N—Q5, Black exchanges Knights (. . . KNxQN) opening up the diagonal for the "Dragon" Bishop. When attacked by P—K5, the King Knight generally retreats to K1—though there are cases, when Black's position is generally aggressive, calling for . . . N—K5. Sometimes, after White has loosened up his position with P—KB4, Black can venture . . . N—KN5, uncovering his "Dragon" Bishop's powerful diagonal. However, this discovered attack involves tactical refinements which have to be studied very carefully by Black.

The QUEEN KNIGHT plays to QB3, where it cooperates with the "Dragon" Bishop in exerting pressure against Q5 (White's Q4). This Knight often plays to the powerful outpost QB5, arriving there via QR4 or K4. At QB5 the Knight is aggressively posted and often serves as the spearhead of Black's pressure along the half-open Queen Bishop file. When White finds the pressure too annoying, he may drive the intruding Knight away with P—QN3; but in that case his position on the Queen Bishop file and on the long diagonal has been rendered somewhat insecure.

The KING BISHOP (the "Dragon" Bishop) is "fianchettoed" to KN2 after the preliminary . . . P—KN3. From this square the Bishop strikes along the diagonal with a masked menace against White's Knight at Q4, his other Knight at QB3 and his Pawn at QN2. The Bishop often plays an aggressive role, and this is especially true when White castles Queen-side and the Bishop consequently has direct threats against White's King. In the event that Black is subjected to direct King-side attack, the "Dragon" Bishop is a useful bulwark of defense.

The QUEEN BISHOP has a more varied role than his colleague. His most favorable spot is doubtless at K3, where he supports the contemplated freeing thrust . . . P—Q4 and also supports the Queen Knight at the outpost QB5. In fact, there are times when the Queen Bishop acts as outpost at QB5. The development . . . B—Q2 is also feasible, but it has a conservative cast which is not in keeping with Black's aggressive mood when playing the Dragon Variation.

The KING ROOK comes to KB1 via castling. The role of this

piece is not too well defined. Generally it will play to Q1 in the event that the Queen file is opened by means of . . . P—Q4; or else it may play to K1 to avoid the exchange of the valuable "Dragon" Bishop where White has played B—K3 and Q—Q2 with a view to B—KR6, forcing the exchange of Bishops (see Clareus-Lynn for an example of this theme). Aside from these possibilities, the King Rook generally remains at KB1 during the middle game.

The QUEEN ROOK, on the other hand, is destined for important action. As a rule it plays to QB1 (except on those occasions when the square QB1 is preempted by the Queen, as in Sköld-Lundin). Here it exerts pressure along the half-open Queen Bishop file, often supporting a Knight at the formidable outpost QB5. From QB1 the Rook also menaces—indirectly, it is true—White's Pawn at QB2. Indirect though this pressure may be, it often persists into the endgame, and it has the effect of inhibiting White's Queen Knight from straying from QB3. This pressure also has the psychological effect of tying down White's Queen to the protection of the Pawn at QB2 (Black's QB7). Black may well be complacent when he achieves this effect, since his own Queen is not similarly hampered.

The QUEEN is employed mostly on the Queen-side. She is posted frequently at QB2, cooperating in the pressure on the half-open Queen Bishop file. Sometimes . . . Q—B1 is played, restraining White from advancing P—KB5 or P—KN4. Sometimes the Queen goes to QR4, after Black's Queen Knight plays to QR4 and is captured by a White Knight at QN3. The recapture . . . QxN brings the Black Queen to QR4. Sometimes (and this is particularly true of situations in which White has played P—KB4 and weakened his position on the diagonal which leads from Black's QR2 to his KN8) Black can bring his Queen to QN3 with considerable effect. Thus we see that the Black Queen has many aggressive possibilities, in keeping with the generally aggressive character of the Dragon Variation.

Review: Salient objectives for Black

(1) "Dragon" Bishop functions powerfully on the long diagonal.

(2) Black's Queen Knight generally occupies powerful outpost at QB5 (after . . . N—QR4 or . . . N—K4).

(3) Black's Queen Rook strikes along the half-open Queen Bishop file.

(4) Freedom achieved by . . . P—Q4 whenever possible.

(5) Whenever White Knight leaves Q4, Black plays . . . B—K3. Ensuing P—KB4 (intending P—B5) best met by . . . Q—B1.

CHAPTER 9

DRAGON VARIATION

III

Black Concludes With a Stunning Queen Sacrifice

THE DRAGON VARIATION calls for sharp play on the part of Black. But the same obligation falls on White as well.

In the following game White stumbles at move 10. His misdeed seems a very slight one, yet he soon finds that he has forfeited the initiative. Black operates on the half-open Queen Bishop file; he gets his outpost at QB5; the "Dragon" Bishop takes a hand in the proceedings; White's development lags.

"Suddenly" a stunning Queen sacrifice cuts short any thought of further resistance on White's part. Study of the game shows that Black's sacrifice, for all its brilliant quality, is merely a part of the evolution of a "Dragon"—planned middle game!

SICILIAN DEFENSE

BUDAPEST, 1933

WHITE	BLACK
G. Meszaros	*I. Wessel*
1 P—K4	P—QB4
2 N—KB3	N—QB3
3 P—Q4	PxP
4 NxP	N—B3
5 N—QB3	P—Q3
6 B—K2	P—KN3

This and Black's following move are thematic to the Dragon Variation.

77

7	Castles	B—N2
8	B—K3	Castles

DIAGRAM 51

(after 8 . . . Castles)
Black's "Dragon" Bishop exerts pressure on the long diagonal.

9 N—N3   . . . .

White removes his Queen Knight from the jurisdiction of the
"Dragon" Bishop and also restrains Black from playing the
freeing move . . . P—Q4.

The text has a possible drawback: as a rule, Knights are not
too well placed at QN3 as they do not command too much of
the vital center area. The Knight, being a short-stepping piece,
must be near the center to function effectively.

The further course of the game illustrates this point very
impressively.

9 . . . .   P—QR3

Black has the ambitious idea of . . . P—QN4 followed
by . . . B—N2, in which case Black would have both fianchettoed Bishops trained powerfully on White's center.

An alternative method, and by far the most popular in recent
years, is 9 . . . B—K3; 10 P—B4, Q—B1 (see Sköld-Lundin).

Figure 6

*One of the most common maneuvers in the DRAGON VARIATION
is the retreat of White's Queen Knight from Q4 to QN3 (generally,
with a view to preventing . . . P—Q4). However, experience
shows that White accomplishes very little with this decentralizing
of his Knight.*

> 10 P—QR4   . . . .

An instinctive reaction: he prevents . . . P—QN4. But since
Black has other ways of developing, the text offers nothing
positive and amounts in the end to loss of time.

White does better to think of the moves that have to be
played in any event—the moves that fit into the opening pattern. In this case one of the indicated moves is B—B3, in order
to guard the King Pawn as a preparation for the aggressive occupation of the center by N—Q5.

DIAGRAM 52

(after 10 P—QR4)
White is reluctant to allow the
contemplated . . . P—QN4.

But the immediate B—B3 is lifeless because Black can counter strongly with . . . N—K4. He can then continue with . . .
NxB *ch* (obtaining the positional advantage of two Bishops
against Bishop and Knight), or with . . . N—B5 (establishing a powerful outpost in the open Queen Bishop file, as in the
game Scheltinga-Landau, p. 119).

From this we conclude that if White wants to play B—B3,
he must precede it with P—B4. This is an important move, giving White control of the valuable square K5. . . . N—K4 is
rendered impossible, and at the same time P—K5 (expansion
in the center) becomes potentially feasible.

Thus, when White avoids P—B4 and neglects control of the
center, Black has noticeable freedom of action (. . . N—K4);
when White controls the center (P—B4), Black's freedom of
action diminishes perceptibly (. . . N—K4 is not possible).

To sum up, after 10 P—B4, P—QN4; 11 B—B3, B—N2
White has a powerful game. (*See Diagram 53.*)

In this position White might try a forceful expansion in the
center by way of 12 P—K5 ! ?, PxP; 13 N—B5 ! creating serious
tactical difficulties for Black.

We return now to the actual game after 10 P—QR4.

(*Diagram for Variation*)

DIAGRAM 53

White has an aggressive formation.

10 . . . .   **B—K3**

Black simply continues his development.

DIAGRAM 54

(after 10 . . . B—K3)
White's initiative is spent.

Now it is not easy to find a promising continuation for
White.

If 11 P—R5 ? (to prevent . . . N—QR4) there follows 11
. . . BxN; 12 PxB, NxRP and Black has won a Pawn.

11 N—Q5 ? also loses a Pawn (11 . . . NxP).

11 P—B4 prevents . . . N—K4 but allows 11 . . . N—QR4 (threatening . . . N—B5); 12 NxN, QxN leading to a perfectly satisfactory game for Black, similar to that of the actual continuation.

(*We return now to the position of Diagram 54.*)

       11   N—Q4   . . . .

A grievous loss of time, completely negating the effects of 9 N—N3. This loss of two tempi by the Knight will leave Black ahead in development!

       11   . . . .   NxN
       12   BxN   Q—R4

DIAGRAM 55

(after 12 . . . Q—R4)
White is condemned to passivity.

What will be Black's plan in this position? He is ahead in development, and is ready to deploy his Rooks. Where? On the half-open Queen Bishop file, of course. The pressure on this file will create an uncomfortable situation for White, as White's Pawn at QB2 is a potential target for attack.

It is impossible to say just what this pressure will lead to, but this much is clear: whatever initiative there is in this position is in Black's hands. We may therefore reasonably conclude that the defense has been quite satisfactory and that Black can face the future with confidence.

13   P—B4   QR—B1

Played according to plan.

The only halfway aggressive idea at White's disposal is 14 P—K5. But after 14 P—K5, PxP; 15 BxKP, KR—Q1 Black has increased his advantage in development and has another open file for his Rooks. And after 14 P—K5, PxP; 15 PxP, N—Q2 White's isolated King Pawn is condemned to death.

14   B—B3   . . . .

Possibly with some notion of playing P—K5 or N—Q5. But now Black sets up his outpost at QB5 with good effect.

14   . . . .   R—B5 *!*

DIAGRAM 56

(after 14 . . . R—B5 *!*)
There are combinations in the air!

Interestingly enough, no sooner does Black set up the thematic outpost at QB5 than the "Dragon" Bishop suddenly takes a hand in the proceedings.

If, for example, White wants to drive away the intrusive Rook, we get this variation: 15 B—K2, RxB *!;* 16 QxR, N—N5 *!*

(discovering an attack on White's Queen by the "Dragon" Bishop) and Black's all-powerful Bishops assure him a winning advantage:

I. 17 Q—Q3, Q—B4 *ch;* 18 K—R1, N—B7 *ch;* 19 RxN,* QxR and Black has much the better game because of his two Bishops powerfully trained on White's Queen-side.

II. 17 P—K5, PxP; 18 Q—K4 (if 18 PxP, BxP; 19 Q—K4, BxP *ch;* 20 K—R1, Q—R4; 21 BxN, BxB and the discovered check will kill White), Q—N3 *ch;* 19 K—R1, QxP and White is helpless against the triple threat of . . . N—B7 *ch* or . . . QxR or . . . QxN.

What is more important than the analytical details of these variations is the way in which Black's Bishops bear down irresistibly on White's vulnerable Queen-side.

(*We return now to the position of Diagram 56.*)

15   R—K1   N—N5 *!*

Again the "Dragon" Bishop announces his presence!

DIAGRAM 57

(after 15 . . . N—N5 *!*)
The "Dragon" Bishop is un-
masked!

With White's King Rook on K1 instead of on KB1, the situation is much more critical for White. If 16 BxB *?,* Q—B4 *ch;* 17

---

* White must avoid smothered mate: 19 K—N1, N—R6 *ch;* 20 K—R1, Q—N8 *ch ! !;* 21 RxQ, N—B7 mate!

K—B1, Q—B7 mate; or 17 K—R1, N—B7 *ch;* 18 K—N1, N—R6 *ch;* 19 K—R1, Q—N8 *ch!!;* or 17 B—Q4, RxB and no matter what White plays, his Queen must go lost by discovered check.*

(*We return now to the position of Diagram 57.*)

16   N—K2 ?   . . . .

"Relatively" better was 16 BxN, BxB *ch;* 17 K—R1, BxB; 18 QxB, BxN; 19 PxB, QxBP with an easy win for Black.

16   . . . .   RxB *! !*

Black, as we shall see, is thoroughly justified in relying on the power of the "Dragon" Bishop.

17   NxR   . . . .

DIAGRAM 58

(after 17 NxR)
Black has a decisive Queen sacrifice!

17   . . . .   QxR *ch ! !*

This stunning Queen sacrifice is the real explanation of Black's previous move. It is all done for the greater glory of the "Dragon" Bishop.

18   QxQ   BxN *ch*

* For discovered check, see *Winning Chess*, p. 80.

DIAGRAM 59

(after 18 . . . BxN *ch*)
The "Dragon" Bishop winds
up the combination.

White has a Queen for two minor pieces, and yet he is helpless against the "Dragon" Bishop!

If now 19 K—B1, B—B5 *ch;* 20 B—K2, NxP mate! Or 19
K—B1, B—B5 *ch;* 20 Q—K2, BxQ *ch* and Black comes out a
piece to the good.

19 K—R1   N—B7 *ch*
    Resigns

For after 20 K—N1 the discovered check 20 . . . N—Q6 *ch*
wins White's Queen and leaves Black a piece ahead.

This sprightly little game has a number of important morals. It
shows, in the first place, that White must develop purposefully in
the Dragon Variation and cannot afford the luxury of second-rate
moves. The game also proves that Black's outpost at QB5 plays a
vital tactical as well as strategical role. And finally, the game rein-
forces in a vivid way the impression that the "Dragon" Bishop,
though masked, is always lurking in the background, waiting for a
suitable opportunity to play a decisive part in Black's counterplay.

CHAPTER 10

DRAGON VARIATION

IV

Vigorous Counterattack

THERE are games in which the approach of the crisis must be watched with the greatest care. Overlook the crisis, or underestimate it, and you may find your game hopeless.

In this game the crisis comes on the tenth move. If Black allows his position to be encircled by the threatened P—B5, he will be left with a difficult and perhaps hopeless game.

Luckily Black does realize the critical nature of the situation. He reacts vigorously, and thus assures himself a promising middle game in which he gradually assumes the initiative.

We see here the intimate connection between opening and middle game. A failure of nerve in the opening stage may render the ensuing middle game hopeless. An incisive, courageous acceptance of the challenge of the opening will, contrariwise, lead to good prospects in the middle game. The Dragon Variation is particularly rich in such critical decisions.

SICILIAN DEFENSE
STOCKHOLM, 1947

WHITE	BLACK
K. Sköld	*E. Lundin*
1 P—K4	P—QB4
2 N—KB3	N—QB3
3 P—Q4	PxP
4 NxP	N—B3

87

5	N—QB3	P—Q3
6	B—K2	P—KN3
7	Castles	B—N2

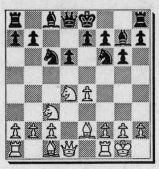

DIAGRAM 60

(after 7 . . . B—N2)
Black's "Dragon" Bishop is
ready for action.

This setting for the Dragon Variation has now become familiar to us. Black's "Dragon" Bishop on KN2 strikes powerfully along the great diagonal, and particularly at White's Q4. Hence White's retreat on the following move:

8	N—N3	. . . .

Getting out of the jurisdiction of the "Dragon" Bishop and also avoiding any awkwardness resulting from a pin by . . . Q—N3 after White plays P—B4.

8	. . . .	Castles
9	B—K3	B—K3
10	P—B4	. . . .

It is not easy for Black to find a suitable continuation here.

In earlier times, the standard continuation was 10 . . . N—QR4, playing for the establishment of the customary outpost at QB5. However, it was found that after 11 P—B5, B—B5; 12 NxN, BxB; 13 QxB, QxN; 14 P—KN4 ! Black's game is

extremely uncomfortable. The Pawn-storming attack leaves
Black with no really satisfactory counterplay, and he is thus
burdened with a dreary position in which passive defense is
his only course.

Eventually the masters were forced to conclude, on the basis
of disheartening experience, that 10 . . . N—QR4 would have
to be discarded.

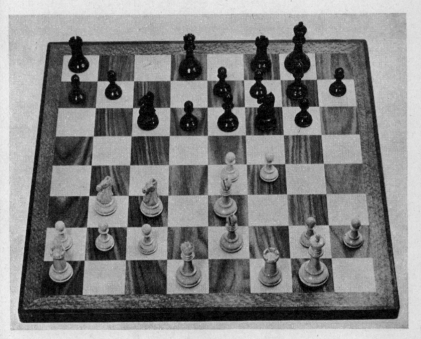

Figure 7

Black is confronted with one of the gravest problems in the
DRAGON VARIATION: how to maintain the centralized *position*
of his Bishop at K3.

10 . . . .   **Q—B1** *!*

The possibilities are now too complex for Black to formulate
a detailed plan. But he can see this far ahead: White's P—B5

DIAGRAM 61

(after 10 P—B4)
White's contemplated ad-
vance of the King Bishop
Pawn threatens to be annoying.

is to be restrained, and . . . P—Q4 is to be forced sooner or
later. Where . . . P—Q4 turns out to be impossible, Black will
concentrate on enhancing the scope of the "Dragon" Bishop.

DIAGRAM 62

(after 10 . . . Q—B1 !)
Black has prevented the trou-
blesome advance of the King
Bishop Pawn.

Black's Queen move has two important functions: it prevents P—B5 and it also prevents P—N4. Thus Black obtains a
breathing spell for developing his game and organizing some

counterthreats before he is annoyed by either P—B5 or P—N4.

White's plan, of course, should center about trying to force either or both of these Pawn thrusts. But he is hampered by the fact that his off-side Knight at QN3 has nothing to contribute to any vital action along these lines.

11   P—KR3   . . . .

This move threatens, or seems to threaten, P—N4.

11 . . . .   R—Q1 !

DIAGRAM 63

(after 11 . . . R—Q1 !)
Black plans action in the center.

Black's last move, made possible by 10 . . . Q—B1 !, is based on a very important idea: *a wing thrust can be parried effectively by a center thrust.*

The specific application of this important principle in the present situation is that if White ventures 12 P—N4, Black counters with 12 . . . P—Q4 !

In that case, 13 PxP can be answered by 13 . . . NxQP and Black has opened up the game very favorably.

Or if 13 P—K5, N—K5 !; 14 NxN, PxN; 15 Q—K1, P—KN4 ! undermining White's King Pawn and remaining with a strong initiative.

(*We return now to the position of Diagram 63.*)

12   B—B3   . . . .

Displeased with the above variations, White concentrates on preventing . . . P—Q4.

12   . . . .   B—B5 !

DIAGRAM 64

(after 12 . . . B—B5 !)
Black has an important advance in mind.

13   R—B2   P—K4 !

Instead of waiting passively for White to carry out his plan of playing P—N4 and P—B5, Black advances strongly in the center.

The advance of Black's King Pawn makes an unpleasant impression at first glance, because it closes the diagonal of the "Dragon" Bishop and creates a backward Queen Pawn.

Yet these drawbacks are more apparent than real. In the first place, the possibility that Black's Queen Pawn can advance to Q4 is by no means ruled out. In the second place, the "Dragon" Bishop's diagonal can only be closed permanently in the event that White exchanges Pawns in the center; but in that case Black takes over the open Queen file and also gets a powerful

DIAGRAM 65

(after 13 . . . P—K4 *!*)
A crucial question: is Black's
advance of the King Pawn
strong or weak?

outpost at Q5 for his Knight—not to mention the fact that his
backward Queen Pawn has been liquidated!

And of course one of the great virtues of 13 . . . P—K4 *!* is
that it forces some kind of crucial decision regarding the Pawn
center: whether White captures now, or allows Black to capture, the possibility of White's playing P—B5 is permanently
ruled out. Thus Black is relieved of further worry about the
one serious menace which has been hanging over his head ever
since the middle game planning began.

14   R—Q2   . . . .

He realizes that 14 P—B5 can be answered powerfully by
14 . . . P—Q4 *!;* hence he concentrates on the backward
Queen Pawn—sane, sensible, logical procedure. But Black
knows how to take suitable countermeasures.

14   . . . .   PxP
15   BxBP   N—K4 *!*

Calmly leaving the seemingly weak Queen Pawn in the
lurch. Actually Black is resourcefully aware of his counterchances. How these counterchances arise is interesting: by

playing 14 . . . PxP Black created a valuable square at K4 for
his Queen Knight. This is one of the most important center
squares, and the Knight's possession of it is all the more dominating because of the fact that *he cannot be driven away by a
White Pawn.*

DIAGRAM 66

(after 15 . . . N—K4 *!*)
A puzzling position for White.

Just how White is to handle this position is quite puzzling.
There does not seem to be any way to proceed advantageously!
The proof:

I. 16 RxP *?* (the most obvious), RxR; 17 QxR, NxB *ch;* 18
PxN, QxP and Black has a winning game because of White's
broken-up King-side. Thus we see that pouncing on the apparently weak Queen Pawn confers no blessings. Suppose, then,
White tries other ways.

II. 16 N—Q5 *?* (to occupy an apparently strong outpost),
NxB *ch;* 17 QxN, NxN; 18 PxN, BxNP winning a Pawn with no
compensation for Black.

III. 16 B—K2, BxB and Black obtains strong pressure: 17
RxB, N—B5; 18 B—B1. Here Black's powerful outpost at QB5
functions with ideal power. Worse yet for White (after 17
. . . N—B5) is 18 R—N1, NxNP *!* again winning a Pawn.

IV. 16 BxN, PxB; 17 RxR *ch,* QxR; 18 QxQ *ch,* RxQ; 19
N—R5, B—QR3; 20 R—Q1, RxR *ch;* 21 BxR, B—B1 (the

"Dragon" Bishop takes a new diagonal). Despite the simplifications, Black has the better of it: his backward Queen Pawn has disappeared and his Bishops have long diagonals.

White still has equality, but the position is *psychologically* discouraging: the much-vaunted initiative conferred by the first move has completely disappeared. In such positions a player can easily become rattled because he finds it difficult to reconcile himself to the fading away of the prospects to which he considers himself entitled.

(*We return now to the position of Diagram 66.*)

| 16 | K—R1 | . . . . |

This noncommittal move is clear indication that White is at a loss for a meaningful continuation and waits for Black to give him his cue.

| 16 | . . . . | N—K1 |

He gives the backward Queen Pawn additional protection and opens the "Dragon" Bishop's diagonal.

17	N—Q4	Q—QB4
18	B—K3	Q—R4
19	N—N3	Q—B2

DIAGRAM 67

(after 19 . . . Q—B2)
Black has improved the position of his Queen.

Black's Queen moves have not been as meaningless as they seemed. White's King Knight is back on its useless post at QN3, his Bishop at K3 no longer bears down indirectly on the backward Queen Pawn.

The position of Black's Queen (on QB2 instead of on QB1) has been improved for reasons that will soon become clear.

At first sight it seems that White has a good move in 20 N—Q5 occupying a strong outpost. But this impression is deceptive: after 20 N—Q5, BxN; 21 RxB, NxB; 22 PxN, BxP Black has won a Pawn.

(We return now to the position of Diagram 67.)

20	R—B2	P—N3
21	B—Q4	QR—B1
22	B—K2	P—Q4 !

Black rids himself of the backward Queen Pawn and at the same time opens up the Queen file for his King Rook. The text signifies complete liberation for Black.

DIAGRAM 68

(after 22 . . . P—Q4 !)
Black has achieved emancipation!

23	PxP	BxP
24	NxB	RxN

DIAGRAM 69

(after 24 . . . RxN)
White is definitely on the defensive.

Now that Black's Rook is functioning effectively on the
newly-opened Queen file, White may expect some uncomfortable moments from the pin * on his Bishop at Q4.

To render his position secure, White should now support the
pinned Bishop with 25 P—B3. Instead, in his haste to extricate
himself from the pin, he runs headlong into a vicious attack.

25   Q—KB1 ?   N—Q3 !

A powerful move which White has overlooked or under-
estimated. The immediate threat is . . . N—K5 or . . . N—B4
with the ugly possibility of forking ** White's King and Queen
by . . . N—N6 ch.

White's position is much more difficult than it appears to be
at first sight.

Suppose he tries 26 B—KB3, attacking Black's Rook on the
Queen file. Then we get 26 . . . RxB !; 27 NxR, NxB; 28 NxN,
N—K5 ! The double threat of 29 . . . N—N6 ch and 29 . . .
NxR ch regains the exchange for Black, and in addition the
"Dragon" Bishop swings into action as Black winds up with 30

* For the pin, see Winning Chess, p. 7.
** For the fork, see Winning Chess, p. 29.

DIAGRAM 70

(after 25 . . . N—Q3 *!*)
White is at a loss for a good
move.

. . . BxP, winning a Pawn and leaving White's Queen-side
Pawns in a split, hopelessly compromised state. This variation
is enormously interesting to students of the Dragon system; for
all the tactical curlicues amount to nothing more than a preparation for 30 . . . BxP. The "Dragon" Bishop has the last
word!

Or if 26 BxN, BxB; 27 B—B3 (there is no time for 27 P—B3,
as 27 . . . N—K5 *!* wins the exchange), N—B4 *!*; 28 Q—B1,
R/Q4—Q1. Black has a winning position, as all his pieces are
admirably posted for aggression, while White's pieces are miserably placed. One possibility is 29 P—B3, B—N6; 30 R—B2,
B—B5; 31 Q—K1, N—N6 *ch;* 32 K—N1, R—K1 and White is
lost, for example 33 Q—Q1, B—K6 *ch;* 34 K—R2, N—B8
dbl ch and mate next move.

(*We return now to the position of Diagram 70.*)

26   **B—R6**   . . . .

Foreseeing the loss of the exchange, White plays to win the
exchange himself. The sequel works out as anticipated—up to
a point!

26   . . . .   **N—K5** *!*

Threatening the gruesome fork . . . N—N6 *ch.*

27	K—N1	NxR
28	BxR	. . . .

If he captures the Knight on KB2, Black moves away his attacked Rook and remains the exchange ahead.

Or if 28 BxN/K5, NxP *ch;* 29 PxN, RxB; 30 BxR, QxB and White is lost because of the hopelessly exposed position of his King.

DIAGRAM 71

(after 28 BxR)
Stealthy but powerful intervention by the "Dragon" Bishop.

28	. . . .	N—K5

For reasons that will at once become clear, this involves threats which in the long run cannot be parried.

White no longer has any satisfactory defense: thus if 29 B—N4, NxB (threatening mate) wins a piece for Black.

Or if 29 BxN, BxB keeping White's Bishop under attack while threatening the brutal 30 . . . B—R7 *ch;* 31 K—R1, N—N6 *ch* winning the Queen. (Again the "Dragon" Bishop has the last word!)

29	B—R6	. . . .

Now comes a brusquely decisive attack.

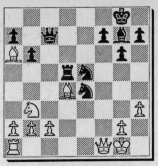

DIAGRAM 72

(after 29 B—R6)
Black is ready for the final
onslaught.

29 . . . .   RxB !
30 NxR   N—N5 !

The crushing point of Black's sacrifice of the exchange.

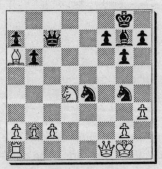

DIAGRAM 73

(after 30 . . . N—N5 !)
Black threatens mate on the
move!

This is an instance of double attack: * Black threatens 31
. . . Q—R7 mate and also 31 . . . BxN *ch;* 32 K—R1, N—N6

* For double attack, see *Winning Chess*, p. 50.

mate. Again we see that Black's combination derives from the power of the "Dragon" Bishop on the diagonal.

Now as to White's defenses: if he tries 31 PxN, then 31 . . . BxN *ch;* 32 K—R1, N—N6 *ch* wins the Queen.

If 31 N—B3 (preventing mate and saving the Knight), then Black wins by utilizing the device of the "overworked piece": * 31 . . . B—Q5 *ch!!* In that case, 32 NxB is answered by 32 . . . Q—R7 mate and 32 K—R1 is met by 32 . . . N—N6 mate.

(*We return now to the position of Diagram 73.*)

31	Q—Q3	. . . .

Now Black wins the Queen by force!

DIAGRAM 74

(after 31 Q—Q3)
White's Queen is lost!

31	. . . .	Q—R7 *ch*
32	K—B1	Q—R8 *ch*
33	K—K2	QxP *ch !*
	Resigns	

White has the choice between:

I. 34 K—K1, Q—B7 *ch;* 35 K—Q1, N—K6 *ch;* 36 K—B1, Q—K8 *ch* and mate next move.

* For the overworked piece, see *Winning Chess,* p. 89.

DIAGRAM 75

(after 33 . . . QxP *ch* !)
Checkmate or win of White's
Queen!

II. 34 K—Q1, Q—N8 *ch* (34 . . . N—B7 *ch* winning the
Queen, is of course good enough); 35 Q—B1 (if 35 K—K2,
Q—B7 *ch* forces the previous variation), N—K6 *ch* winning
the Queen.

This game illustrates the enormous power of the "Dragon"
Bishop when the Black forces are skillfully managed—note the
large number of variations in which the scope of this Bishop is convincingly evidenced.

In addition, 10 . . . Q—B1 ! is shown to be an immensely valuable move in neutralizing White's contemplated Pawn-storming
attack (P—B5 followed by P—N4).

11 . . . R—Q1 ! is also important because of the resulting possibility of advancing Black's King Pawn or Queen Pawn according
to circumstances. By keeping the center fluid Black underlines the
power of the "Dragon" Bishop.

CHAPTER 11

DRAGON VARIATION

V

White's Queen-side Castling Proves a Fiasco

No SYSTEM of chess teaching can provide for every contingency. Yet there are two vital factors which can guide you when confronted with unexpected moves. One is the confidence you have from knowing that the line you have chosen—Dragon Variation— is essentially sound against all possible lines and has stood the test of time for decades. The other important factor is this: when a surprise move turns up, you must be prepared to look for the weakness which lurks behind the flashy appearance of the unexpected move.

In the following game, it is White's Queen-side castling which furnishes the surprise. But, as we shall see, the sturdy Dragon Variation is not to be bowled over by this brash line of play. What is even more interesting is that Black quickly puts his finger on the essential weakness of White's Queen-side castling: *the vulnerable position of White's King.*

Far from being taken aback, the player of the Black pieces immediately adjusts himself to the situation and unleashes an irresistible attack. The result is a crashing victory for the Dragon Variation, and a game which is extremely valuable for the student.

SICILIAN DEFENSE
POSTAL GAME, 1945

WHITE	BLACK
B. Clareus	*A. G. Lynn*
1 P—K4	P—QB4

2	N—KB3	P—Q3
3	P—Q4	PxP
4	NxP	N—KB3
5	N—QB3	P—KN3
6	B—KN5	. . . .

DIAGRAM 76

(after 6 B—KN5)
White plans Queen-side castling!

White's last move is one that we have not encountered previously. That is because he is following a different plan this time: he intends to *castle on the Queen-side*. He therefore mobilizes his Queen-side forces more rapidly than he would ordinarily, when contemplating King-side castling.

6	. . . .	B—N2
7	Q—Q2	N—B3
8	Castles	Castles

We have now reached a point where we can fruitfully inquire into the logic behind White's Queen-side castling.

As we have seen earlier, the possibility of Pawn captures and recaptures is a very important factor in planning the course of a game. *These captures and recaptures result in line-opening.* And this line-opening in turn creates highways for the movements of our forces in aggressive mood.

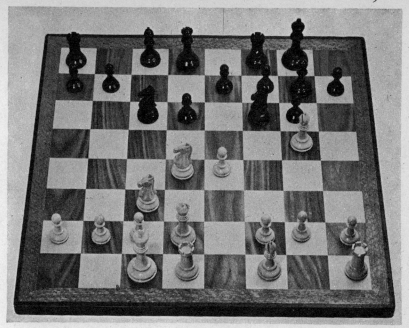

Figure 8

White's castling Queen-side in any line of the DRAGON VARIA-
TION is a warning that he contemplates an all-out attack. The en-
suing play will call for hair-sharp timing on both sides.

In this case, White's basic tactical idea is to play P—KR4
and P—KR5 followed by PxP, taking advantage of the fact
that Black's King Knight Pawn is at KN3. Once White has
played to KR5, he is certain of opening the King Rook file, and
having the Black King's address (at White's KN8) he will
muster his heavy artillery on the newly-opened King Rook file
to operate against Black's King.

To carry out this idea, White needs to play P—KN4 as well
(to support the King Rook Pawn on KR5). This advance in
turn requires the protective advance P—KB3. White's policy,
then, is a Pawn-storming attack on the King-side. Given this
policy, it would be foolish for White to castle King-side: his

King would only be in the way of his pieces, and in fact might even be exposed to dangerous counterattack after the advance of White's Pawns. According to this line of reasoning, White's King is much safer at QB1—hence Queen-side castling.

DIAGRAM 77

(after 8 . . . Castles)
What is White's attacking plan?

9   N—N3   . . . .

This is the usual move made by White to avoid any tactical tricks due to the fact that White's Knight at Q4 was directly attacked by Black's Knight at QB3 and indirectly attacked by the "Dragon" Bishop at KN2.

So far we have studied the situation only from White's point of view. He means to execute a Pawn-storming attack against Black's King. What does Black intend to do about this threat? What are Black's resources?

The answers to these questions will give us the complete details of Black's plan for the rest of the game.

In the first place, from the narrow aspect of passive defense, Black's "Dragon" Bishop is a tower of strength. Thus, if White opens the King Rook file and posts his Queen at KR2, he does not threaten Q—R8 mate because the "Dragon" Bishop at KN2 guards the square KR1 (KR1 in Black's camp, KR8 in White's).

DIAGRAM 78

(after 9 N—N3)
What resources does Black
have for counterattack?

Of course, this "threat" is not very menacing at the moment, for to execute it White requires no less than seven moves. But it would be foolish for Black to be lulled into a sense of security because of the remoteness of the threat. The sensible reaction is: "White needs seven moves to carry out his threat. *What can I do in the meantime?*"

Black's first concrete conclusion is that he must be careful to guard his precious "Dragon" Bishop from removal by exchange.

Black's second conclusion is that he must utilize the precious seven moves' grace to initiate a counterattack. With what?

His counterattacking resources are considerable. In the first place, as we have seen in earlier games, the "Dragon" Bishop points directly at White's QN2. Generally this threat is of a strategic nature—but not here. For after White's castling Queen-side, *his King is the target.* His King is not so safe at QB1 after all.

Secondly, as we know from earlier games, Black has an important weapon in the half-open Queen Bishop file. Once he places a Rook at QB1, he exerts pressure on White's Knight at QB3 (already menaced by the "Dragon" Bishop) and thence on White's Pawn at QB2. But here again this generally strate-gic threat has *tactical* significance: *it is aimed at White's King*.

Third, Black can occupy the outpost at QB5, say by . . . N—K4 and . . . N—B5 (after due preparation). This threat, likewise generally of a strategic character, also becomes *tacti-cal* because of the presence of White's King.

Fourth, when Black plays . . . B—K3, he has a potential menace against White's Queen Rook Pawn. As a rule, this Pawn is guarded by White's Queen Rook. Here this protection is lacking because the Rook is now at Q1.

Fifth, Black has the possibility of advancing his Queen Rook Pawn to QR6. When the Pawn gets to QR5, it will drive away the White Knight now at QN3 which helps to guard White's King. When the Queen Rook Pawn gets to QR6, it will force the removal of White's Queen Knight Pawn from QN2. But this will weaken the position of White's Queen Knight at QB3, already menaced on the long diagonal by the "Dragon" Bishop and on the half-open Queen Bishop file by Black's Queen Rook on QB1.

So we see that Black really has considerable resources for punishing White's King. With White concentrating on smok-ing out Black's King at KN8 and Black concentrating on smok-ing out White's King at QB8, we have a very exciting game in prospect. What matters now is the *timing*. One inexact move may spell the difference between victory and defeat.

(*We return now to the position of Diagram 78.*)

9 . . . .   B—K3

And here is such an inexact move. Black should first play 9 . . . R—K1 *!* so that he can answer 10 B—KR6 with 10 . . . B—R1 *!* retaining the "Dragon" Bishop. (*See Diagram 79.*)

10 K—N1   . . . .

But White is inexact too. Exploiting Black's last move, he should play 10 B—KR6 *!* forcing the removal of Black's valu-

DIAGRAM 79

(after 9 . . . B—K3)
White can dispose of the
"Dragon" Bishop.

able "Dragon" Bishop (obviously 10 . . . B—R1 ? is answered
by 11 BxR winning the exchange).

The text has its points. By playing the King to QN1, White
gives his vulnerable Queen Rook Pawn additional protection.
But he loses an important tempo for attack.

        10 . . . .   R—B1

Again Black is inexact. Intent on prosecuting his counterattack, he neglects to preserve his "Dragon" Bishop by playing
10 . . . R—K1 ! (See Diagram 80.)

        11 P—B3   . . . .

Preparing to begin the Pawn-storming attack with P—N4
followed by P—KR4 and P—R5. But again White has neglected to remove the "Dragon" Bishop by B—KR6.

        11 . . . .   R—K1 !

Now Black is certain of being able to retain the "Dragon"
Bishop as 12 B—KR6 can be answered by 12 . . . B—R1 !
With this vital point established once for all, Black's counter-
attack can flourish. (See Diagram 81.)

DIAGRAM 80

(after 10 . . . R—B1)
Again Black permits the re-
moval   of   the   "Dragon"
Bishop.

DIAGRAM 81

(after 11 . . . R—K1 !)
Now the "Dragon" Bishop is
safe from exchange.

(*We return now to the position of Diagram 81.*)

12   P—N4   N—K4 !

Preparing for the powerful infiltration . . . N—B5; as we
know, occupying this aggressive outpost is one of the key features of Black's policy.

13   B—K2   . . . .

DIAGRAM 82

(after 13 B—K2)
Black is building up menacing
pressure on the Queen-side.

It has already become clear that Black's threats are maturing
much more rapidly than White's. White has not even begun to
force open the King Rook file, while Black is concentrating his
pieces against the White King in a really menacing manner.
Note also that White's Knights are useless as far as participat-
ing in the attack is concerned.

Black can now play 13 . . . N—B5, but instead he hits on a
much more effective move.

(We return now to the position of Diagram 82.)

13   ....   N/B3—Q2 *!*

His idea is to play . . . N—N3, after which he is certain of
keeping a Knight on QB5 no matter how White proceeds. This
is bound to be disastrous for White.

Another useful point about the text is that it unmasks the
"Dragon" Bishop for action against White's King.

14   B—KR6   ....

Too late! (*See Diagram 83.*)

14   ....   B—R1 *!*

DIAGRAM 83

(after 14 B—KR6)
Black naturally avoids the ex-
change of the "Dragon"
Bishop.

Now that Black's King Rook is at K1, he can simply avoid
the exchange of Bishops.

15 P—KR4   . . . .

And this is another case of "too little and too late." Black
simply continues with his own attack. (We no longer call it a
"counterattack," as it is obvious that it is Black who is the real
aggressor.)

15 . . . .   N—N3

Going ahead with his plan of stationing a Knight on QB5.

16 P—R5   N/K4—B5
17 BxN   NxB
18 Q—R2   . . . .

White seems almost on the point of achieving his objective.
His Queen and King Rook are on the King Rook file, which he
is about to open with 19 PxP. But meanwhile Black has placed
his forces in menacing positions and even at this stage he can
shatter his opponent's castled position with 18 . . . NxP.

Instead, he stops for a clever interpolation.

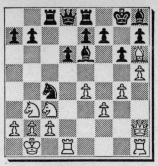

DIAGRAM 84

(after 18 Q—R2)
White's position on the King
Rook file seems to promise a
winning attack.

(We return now to the position of Diagram 84.)

18 . . . .   P—KN4 *! !*

Beautiful play.

DIAGRAM 85

(after 18 . . . P—KN4 *! !*)
Black has prevented the opening of the King Rook file.

Black has paused in his attacking maneuvers to sacrifice a
Pawn *in order to avoid the opening of the King Rook file*.

As is often pointed out in this book, Pawn captures result in line-opening. By playing . . . P—KN4!! Black prevents the opening of the King Rook file and thereby paralyzes the further unfolding of White's attack. The loss of the Pawn is a trifling matter in comparison with the breaking of White's attack.

19 BxP   . . . .

If 19 R—Q3 (to give the Knight at QB3 additional protection) then 19 . . . B—K4! followed by 20 . . . P—B3 puts White's Bishop out of play permanently.

19 . . . .   NxP!

Smashing up White's castled position. The carefully prepared attack now bursts over White's King with murderous force.

DIAGRAM 86

(after 19 . . . NxP!)
White's castled position is
toppling.

20 KxN   RxN!

Even stronger than 20 . . . BxN *ch*—for by threatening the fearsome double check 21 . . . RxN *ch* * Black gains time for increasing the pressure on the Queen Bishop file.

21 K—N1   Q—B2!

* For double check, see *Winning Chess*, p. 85.

Black does not bother with the gain of a Pawn (21 . . .
RxKBP) as he wants to win in the quickest manner.

22 B—B1   P—R4 !

White's protective Knight at N3 must be removed.

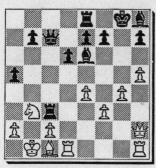

DIAGRAM 87

(after 22 . . . P—R4 !)
White's   protective   Knight
must be removed.

23 Q—Q2   . . . .

23 B—N2 does not help, as Black imperturbably strengthens
his grip on the position with 23 . . . R—QB1 ! and if 24 BxR,
QxB threatening mate. Then, after 25 N—Q4, R—B5 White
would have to cry "uncle."

23 . . . .   P—R5
24 N—Q4   . . . .

White thinks he has closed the terrible long diagonal, but he
is immediately undeceived. The powerful Black Bishops are
too much for him. (*See Diagram 88.*)

24 . . . .   BxP *ch* ! !
25 KxB   Q— B5 *ch*
26 K—R1   . . . .

DIAGRAM 88

(after 24 N—Q4)
Black's powerful Bishops are
admirably posted for attack.

After 26 K—N1 Black works out pretty much the same kind
of finish with 26 . . . P—R6 intending 27 . . . P—R7 *ch.*
26 K—N2 simply loses time (26 . . . P—R6 *ch*).

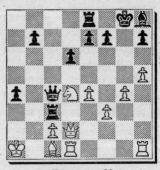

DIAGRAM 89

(after 26 K—R1)
The White King and the
"Dragon" Bishop are on the
same diagonal!

26 . . . .   RxQBP

Taking advantage of the fact that White's Knight is pinned.*

* For the pin, see *Winning Chess*, p. 7.

27	Q—N5 *ch*	K—B1
28	B—N2	RxB *!*
29	KxR	R—B1 *!*

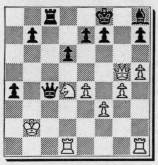

DIAGRAM 90

(after 29 . . . R—B1 *!*)
The "Dragon" Bishop's pin
proves decisive.

Black's chief threat is now 30 . . . Q—N6 *ch;* 31 K—R1,
R—B7. Note that White's Knight, being pinned by the
"Dragon" Bishop, cannot capture the Queen or Rook. He is
therefore helpless against the mate threat.

30 Q—K3 . . . .

Or 30 Q—Q2, Q—N6 *ch;* 31 K—R1, R—B7 winning the
Queen!

30 . . . . Q—N5 *ch*
Resigns

If 31 K—R2, R—B7 *ch !;* 32 NxR, Q—N7 mate (the
"Dragon" Bishop is still cooperating!).

If 31 K—R1, R—B7 (thanks to the "Dragon" Bishop!); 32
R—QN1, BxN *ch* (the "Dragon" Bishop delivers the final
blow!) and mate follows.

From this splendid game we learn that White's attempt to play
for attack by castling Queen-side recoils on him because Black's

DIAGRAM 91

(after 30 . . . Q—N5 *ch*)
White's King has no refuge.

"Dragon" Bishop acquires fearful attacking powers. The Bishop is ably seconded by Black's play in the half-open Queen Bishop file, supplemented by the posting of a Black Knight at QB5.

Bear in mind that in this type of game, *with both players striving for sharp attack*, accurate timing is of the essence. Any move that does not conform to the thematic ideas of the variation may lead to defeat. However, study of this game demonstrates that Black has every reason for confidence in the resources at his disposal.

CHAPTER 12

DRAGON VARIATION

VI

Relentless Positional Pressure by Black

DESPITE its rather sedate course, this game is perhaps our most dynamic example of the Dragon Variation. There is drama in this game, but the tension is well concealed.

On the surface, White seems to have a perfectly satisfactory and even aggressive position. Yet, bit by bit, he is driven back until he finds himself quite helpless in the grip of Black's well-posted pieces.

The dramatic nature of this game becomes apparent only on analysis. Careful examination shows that it is the elements of the Dragon formation that bring about White's downfall. One by one, these elements appear and gain cumulative power, until White's downfall becomes obvious and imminent.

SICILIAN DEFENSE
MATCH, 1939

	WHITE	BLACK
	T. D. van Scheltinga	S. Landau
1	P—K4	P—QB4
2	N—KB3	P—Q3
3	P—Q4	PxP
4	NxP	N—KB3
5	N—QB3	P—KN3
6	B—K2	B—N2
7	Castles	N—B3
8	B—K3	. . . .

DIAGRAM 92

(after 8 B—K3)
White has given his Knight at
Q4 added protection.

White's last move guards his Knight on Q4 from attack by
. . . NxP. (This threat was explained in Giusti-Nutrizio, page
62, where White played 8 N—N3 to parry the threat.)

Not only is 8 B—K3 a useful protective move; it also has the
virtue of developing a new piece.

8 . . . .   Castles
9 P—B4   . . . .

DIAGRAM 93

(after 9 P—B4)
The advance of White's King
Bishop Pawn has pros and
cons.

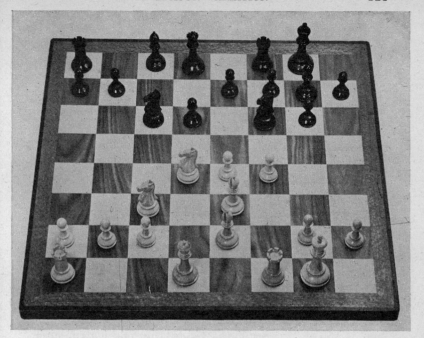

Figure 9

White's P—KB4 is a favorite attacking method in the DRAGON VARIATION. But the advance of the King Bishop Pawn also has its drawbacks if White does not observe due care in neutralizing the power of the "Dragon" Bishop.

This stops Black from freeing himself by . . . P—Q4. However, 9 N—N3 is the approved method of stopping . . . P—Q4 —at least for some time to come.

The advance of White's King Bishop Pawn does not really "prevent" . . . P—Q4; but it effectually discourages Black all the same, for if now 9 . . . P—Q4; 10 P—K5 leaves Black with a very uncomfortable position.

Thus we see that 9 P—B4 is an aggressive move. (It can also have the aggressive point of being combined in a Pawn storm: P—B5 and P—KN4, with the demolition of Black's King-side as the goal of White's advance.)

To a player of moderate strength, the forceful aspect of 9 P—B4 is quite obvious. What is less obvious to such a player— or reader—is that 9 P—B4 weakens White on the diagonal leading to his King (from Black's QR2 to White's KN1) by opening up the diagonal and by removing the Pawn protection previously extended to the Bishop on K3 by the White Pawn on KB2. With the general loosening of White's security on this important diagonal, there is a new shakiness in the position of his Knight on Q4. The Knight is now slightly, but subtly, more vulnerable to threats from Black's "Dragon" Bishop.

It seems logical, therefore, for Black to play 9 . . . Q—N3. The combined action of the Black Queen (on the diagonal QR2—KN8) and the Black King Bishop (on the diagonal KR1—QR8) seems an ideal example of action by the "Dragon" Bishop. Yet, attractive as this combined pressure may seem, it creates problems for *Black* rather than for White!

9 . . . Q—N3 threatens . . . QxP as well as . . . NxP unmasking the power of Black's "Dragon" Bishop. If White proceeds passively against 9 . . . Q—N3, he soon finds himself in trouble, for example 10 Q—Q3, N—KN5 *!* (the "threat" of 10 . . . NxP *?* is now inoperative because of the surprising reply 11 N—Q5 *!* attacking the Queen and winning a piece); 11 N—Q5, BxN *! !;* 12 NxQ, BxB *ch;* 13 K—R1, BxN and with three minor pieces for the Queen, Black is ahead in material.

So far, so good—for Black. But White has a much more enterprising way of meeting 9 . . . Q—N3. In the complicated variation just shown, Black's "Dragon" Bishop plays a great role. Hence White needs a line of play in which the power of the "Dragon" Bishop is minimized or completely wiped out. This is how it is done (after 9 . . . Q—N3): 10 P—K5 *!*, PxP; 11 PxP, NxP; 12 N—B5 *!* (attacking the Queen), QxP; 13 NxP *ch,* K—R1; 14 B—Q4, N—N1; 15 N—N5, Q—N5; 16 N—Q5. White has a terrific initiative at the nominal cost of a Pawn; Black's game is disorganized and his Queen out of play.

It is therefore understandable that Black prefers to by-pass these dubious complications by playing 'possum and choosing a noncommittal continuation.

9 . . . .   B—Q2

Quietly continuing his development and awaiting future developments.

DIAGRAM 94

(after 9 . . . B—Q2)
Black is prepared to begin operations on the half-open Queen Bishop file.

10   K—R1   . . . .

White wants to render himself less vulnerable by moving his King off the dangerous diagonal. But he should be thinking hereabouts about playing N—N3, for reasons that will soon become clear.

10 . . . .   R—B1

Black opened the Queen Bishop file for himself when he played 3 . . . PxP in the opening. Now he develops the Queen Rook to this half-open file, where it exerts pressure against White's Queen Bishop Pawn. For the time being this pressure is masked, but the game can easily take a turn after which the pressure will become direct.

11   B—B3 ?   . . . .

White wants to post his Queen Knight aggressively at Q5 and in order to do this he must first guard his King Pawn. But this plan, laudable as it is, has not been adequately prepared.

The right move was 11 N—N3 and if 11 . . . N—QR4; 12 NxN, QxN; 13 B—B3 with fighting chances for both players.

11 . . . .   N—QR4 *!*

DIAGRAM 95

(after 11 . . . N—QR4 *!*)
Black's Queen Knight is headed for the powerful outpost QB5.

Black's last move indicates that he has formed his plan of the future play by combining thematic elements of the Dragon Variation. Thus, Black has increased his power in the half-open Queen Bishop file by playing to post his Queen Knight at QB5. Here the Knight is really menacing, for he attacks the White Bishop at K3 and also White's Pawn at QN2. Even after these threats are neutralized, the invading Knight is still an unfriendly neighbor, as will be seen.

In addition, Black's Queen Rook will exert powerful pressure on the Queen Bishop file, with White's Queen Bishop Pawn as a welcome target.

Finally, Black will shape the game in such a way that White's Knight on Q4 and his Bishop on KB3 have little scope. This calls for an eventual . . . P—K4 *!*

(We return now to the position of Diagram 95.)

12 B—N1   ....

Eliminating one of White's liabilities. Note that 12 P—
QN3 ? (to prevent . . . N—B5) is out of the question because
of 12 . . . RxN. This is a portent of greater difficulties to
come, in consequence of the Black Rook's power on the half-
open Queen Bishop file.

12 ....   N—B5

The Knight is strongly posted in enemy territory, and 13
. . . NxNP is threatened.

13 P—QN3   ....

He reacts instinctively to the Knight's annoying presence;
but now the Knight becomes even more annoying!

13 ....   N—R6

Exposing White's Knight on QB3 to attack by the Black
Queen Rook. At the same time White's Pawn at QB2, which is
"fixed" on its square, is stamped as a vulnerable target for
attack.

DIAGRAM 96

(after 13 . . . N—R6)
Black has developed strong
pressure along the Queen
Bishop file.

It is not so easy for White to neutralize the hostile pressure on the Queen Bishop file. Thus if 14 N/B3—K2 ? Black wins a piece by 14 . . . P—K4 !

Or if 14 N/Q4—K2, Q—R4; 15 Q—Q3, N—N5 (now the "Dragon" Bishop gets into the act) and Black's pressure on the Queen Bishop file has been powerfully augmented by diagonal pressure as well.

(*We return now to the position of Diagram 96.*)

14   N—N1   . . . .

To retreat the Knight to its original square makes a bad impression. On the other hand, getting rid of Black's obstreperous Knight is a distinct achievement for White.

14   . . . .   NxN
15   RxN   P—K4 !

At first sight this move comes as a surprise because it closes the diagonal of the "Dragon" Bishop. But Black knows what he

DIAGRAM 97

(after 15 . . . P—K4 !)
The scope of White's Knight
will now be sadly limited.

is about: he foresees that there are ways in which this Bishop can come to life again; and his immediate objective is *to de-*

prive White's Knight of any squares on which he can function usefully.

16   N—K2   B—B3

Whereas the mobility of White's Knight has been reduced to a minimum, Black's Queen Bishop has become more active. White's King Pawn requires additional protection.

Note, by the way, that if White now plays 17 BxP *?* he loses a piece: 17 . . . P—N3 *!* cuts off the Bishop's retreat, and 18 . . . Q—B2 wins the Bishop.

17   PxP   . . . .

The alternative 17 Q—Q3 is answered by 17 . . . P—Q4 *!* with a dynamic upsurge of energy in Black's position. The suddenly liquid position of the Pawn center, with its coming exchanges of Pawns, portends new opening of lines; and in particular, the "Dragon" Bishop comes to life again. If 18 KPxP, NxP and Black's pieces are beautifully posted.

White therefore discards 17 Q—Q3 and plays to exchange Queens. This is a sound procedure, because the generally aggressive character of Black's game signifies favorable potentialities for his Queen—whereas the generally lifeless character of White's game signifies a dearth of possibilities for White's Queen. However, Black's positional advantage is so marked that the exchange of Queens does not offer White too much relief.

17   . . . .   PxP
18   QxQ   KRxQ
19   N—N3   . . . .

White's simplifying strategy has not brought him any relief. His Rooks are useless, while Black's Rooks are active. Black's Queen Bishop attacks the King Pawn, and his colleague (the "Dragon" Bishop) can be usefully deployed at KB1 keeping an eye on two good diagonals.

DIAGRAM 98

(after 19 N—N3)
White's Knight is still unfor-
tunately posted.

White's Knight is in a bad way, having no scope to speak of
and being limited to defensive work. The outlook for White
is very poor.

19 . . . .   P—KR4 !

Threatening . . . P—R5 which would win the King Pawn
through the forced removal of the protective Knight. The text
is also part of a long-range policy dedicated to harrying
White's Knight into immobility.

If White now tries 20 BxQRP, Black achieves a very favorable position with 20 . . . R—R1; 21 B—N6, R—Q7 etc.

20   KR—K1   R—Q7
21   BxQRP   RxBP

Black's initiative persists.

22   P—QR4   B—B1 !

Now the "Dragon" Bishop is off his original diagonal, but
there are menacing possibilities all the same. Thus Black
threatens 23 . . . B—N5; 24 R—K3 (on other Rook moves,
the King Pawn goes lost after . . . P—R5), N—Q2 ! cutting
off the retreat of White's Queen Bishop and having in view the
dreadful threat of 25 . . . R—R1 winning the Bishop!

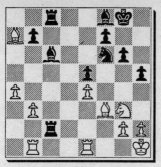

DIAGRAM 99

(after 22 . . . B—B1 !)
White will gradually succumb
to the relentless pressure.

From this point on, Black's Rook on the seventh rank plays
an important role in the gradual increase of the pressure on
White's game.

(*We return now to the position of Diagram 99.*)

23   B—Q1   . . . .

23 B—N1 leaves White's pieces in a jumbled mess; while if
23 B—K3 White must lose a Pawn by retreating his Knight
after 23 . . . P—R5; for if 24 B—N5 ?, N—R2 !; 25 BxP, P—
KN4 winning a piece!

23 . . . .   R—R7

The unwelcome intruder remains on the seventh rank. Black
is still threatening to win the King Pawn by . . . P—R5.

24   QR—B1   . . . .

Pinning * Black's Queen Bishop so that White's King Pawn
is immune from capture.

24 . . . .   P—R5 !
25 N—B1   . . . .

* For the pin, see *Winning Chess*, p. 7.

DIAGRAM 100

(after 25 N—B1)
Black's Rook on the seventh
rank plays a decisive role.

Obviously Black cannot play 25 . . . NxP? because of 26 RxN etc. But Black has a stronger line:

25 . . . .   P—R6 !

For if 26 PxP (or 26 P—KN3) Black wins the exchange with 26 . . . BxP *ch!* *

On 26 B—B3 Black plays 26 . . . PxP *ch;* 27 BxP, R—Q1 with unrelenting pressure. White's position is bound to cave in, as his pieces are tied down and his King Pawn is vulnerable. Black's grip on the position will be strengthened by . . . R—Q6 and ultimately Black should be able to double Rooks on the seventh rank with devastating effect.

What makes all the difference in the world between the prospects of both players is that Black's superior opening development left his pieces in aggressive positions; White's inferior opening development left his pieces in passive, ineffectual positions. This is particularly noticeable if one compares the respective positions of the Rooks.

26 N—N3   RxNP !

* For discovered attack, see *Winning Chess,* p. 67.

Now the threat is 27 . . . NxP *!;* 28 NxN, BxN; 29 RxR, R—K7 *ch* with a debacle for White. Or 27 . . . NxP *!;* 28 RxN, BxR; 29 RxR, RxN *ch* and mate next move.*

27　R—B4　　. . . .

White gives the King Pawn the needed extra protection by putting his Queen Rook on a square where it enjoys protection by another White unit.

To maintain the initiative, Black seizes a new open line:

27　. . . .　　R—Q1 *!*

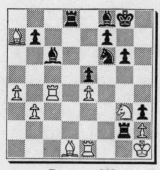

DIAGRAM 101

(after 27 . . . R—Q1 *!*)
White's pieces are tied down
to purely defensive tasks.

Black's last move has *unpinned* his Bishop on QB3. In addition he has threats of . . . R—Q6 or . . . R/Q1—Q7.

28　B—K3　　. . . .

In order to prevent . . . R/Q1—Q7.

28　. . . .　　R—Q6 *!*

The pressure has reached a point where White hardly has a move to his name, for example 29 B—N1, B—R3 followed by

* Discovered check. See *Winning Chess,* p. 80.

DIAGRAM 102

(after 28 . . . R—Q6!)
Black's pressure will soon
yield results.

. . . B—B5 (menacing White's King Pawn) and White cannot last very long.

Or 29 B—N5, RxB; 30 RxR, N—N5 (threatens mate as well
as 31 . . . RxP *ch;* 32 K—N1, R—N7 *ch* and 33 . . . RxN);
31 R—Q2, N—B7 *ch;* 32 RxN, RxR and the threats of . . . R—
QN7 and . . . P—B4 will be decisive.

(*We return now to the position of Diagram 102.*)

29	B—QB2	R/Q6xB *!*
30	RxR	N—N5

DIAGRAM 103

(after 30 . . . N—N5)
Black threatens mate on the
move in two different ways!

31 **R—KB3**   **B—R3**

The "Dragon" Bishop enters upon the scene. Black is now
ready to recover the exchange without any diminution of the
pressure.

DIAGRAM 104

(after 31 . . . B—R3)
The "Dragon" Bishop aug-
ments Black's pressure.

32 **N—B1**   **N—B7** *ch*
33 **RxN**   **RxR**

Black threatens (a) 34 . . . RxN mate; (b) 34 . . . P—B4;
(c) 34 . . . B—Q2 followed by . . . B—N5 and . . . B—
B6 *ch.* And there is still another threat!

(*See Diagram 105.*)

34 **K—N1**   . . . .

There is no way out for White. If 34 N—N3, P—B4; 35 K—
N1, R—N7 *ch;* 36 K—R1, P—B5 winning a piece as in the
game.

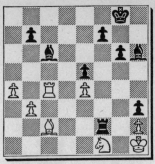

DIAGRAM 105

(after 33 . . . RxR)
Black has four threats!

34	. . . .	R—N7 *ch*
35	K—R1	RxB *!*

DIAGRAM 106

(after 35 . . . RxB *!*)
Black's sacrifice of the exchange wins a piece.

White resigns, for after 36 RxR, BxP *ch* he is a piece down
with a hopeless game.

This encounter has taken an extremely instructive course. Black
carried out one of the most important thematic ideas of the Dragon
Variation by playing his Queen Knight to the valuable outpost

QB5. In his efforts to dislodge the intruder, White lost time and weakened his position. Having a clear initiative, Black steadily improved his game by posting a Rook strongly on the seventh rank and concentrating on White's weak King Pawn.

Appraising the effect of these policies on White's position, we observed that throughout the game his Knights had no scope, his Bishops did not function aggressively, his Rooks were tied down to defensive tasks.

Black's initiative, and White's inability to fight back effectively, may both be traced back to White's inexact play in the opening. He weakened his position on a vital diagonal, he allowed the outpost to be established at his QB4, he did not follow up his development systematically. These seemingly minor faults added up to a catastrophe.

♔ **PART THREE** ♔

Playing With the Black Pieces

Against 1 P—Q4

CHAPTER 13

What Defense Shall I Play
Against 1 P—Q4 . . . ?

In 1927, when Frank Marshall was preparing to sail for London to play in an international master tournament, he approached friends with the half-comic, half-plaintive query: "What defense shall I play against 1 P—Q4 . . . ?" If one of the greatest players in the history of the game felt this way after thirty years, what are lesser mortals to say?

The fact is that finding a defense against 1 P—Q4 is no laughing matter! Most of us have been brought up on 1 P—K4, and we find something uncongenial in the lines of play which evolve from 1 P—Q4. There is not the slightest doubt that 1 P—Q4 leads to just as many—if not more—brilliant possibilities; yet many of us cannot repress a feeling of being at home in the King Pawn openings, and a related feeling of strangeness as regards the Queen Pawn openings. (One of the reasons for recommending the Stonewall Attack for White is the recognition of the prejudice many players have against the Queen Pawn openings!)

Yet this attitude, irrational as it may seem, is grounded in solid fact. The Queen Pawn openings require considerable maneuvering skill, abounding as they do in positional finesses. It is fatally easy for Black to commit some obscure positional mistake early in the game, leaving himself with the bleakest of middle game prospects. Worse yet, there are any number of variations in which he is condemned from the start to a seriously constricted position. And constricted positions, as the great Tarrasch so truly observed, have in themselves the germs of coming defeat.

The worst defect of many Black formations in the Queen's Gambit Declined is the Pawn position. With most of Black's Pawns frequently placed on white squares, the activity of Black's Queen Bishop is so circumscribed that the Bishop is virtually degraded to the status of a Pawn. Here is a case in point:

DIAGRAM 107

Black's Queen Bishop has no scope to speak of.

The mobility of Black's Queen Bishop, hemmed in by its own Pawns, has been so severely reduced that it is hardly an exaggeration to say that Black is practically a piece down for the middle game and the ending. At all events, Black is suffering from an affliction which has not been visited on his opponent. Decades ago the masters became expert at exploiting this type of advantage, and the ability to utilize it has seeped down into the ranks of lesser players.

Should Black, in order to avoid these difficulties, resort to the so-called "irregular defenses"? Should he consult an opening manual to study the Nimzoindian, Queen's Indian, King's Indian, or Gruenfeld Defenses? Excellent as these lines of play are, they have the grave drawback, from our point of view, that their proper handling requires a minute knowledge of the fine points of position play, not to mention thorough familiarity with a great number of variations.

We come back, then, to the idea of declining the Queen's Gambit and, if possible, *avoiding the constricted type of middle game position which it generally involves for Black.* Is there a defense which avoids this difficulty? There is such a defense, and it is known as Lasker's Defense.

The object of this defense is *simplification.* From the very start Black has in view the exchange of several pieces. These exchanges free his game by ridding him of pieces that past experience tells us will have little mobility. And *these* Black

Figure 10

Note the magnificent development of Black's "problem" Bishop to KN5, which is characteristic of LASKER'S DEFENSE. Compare this with the miserable situation of the same Bishop in Diagram 107.

pieces are to be exchanged against White pieces which, as we likewise know from experience, will have considerably more mobility than their Black opposite numbers.

In each example of Lasker's Defense, then, Black's strategical plan is based on simplification. Black proceeds on the theory that once he has carried out several exchanges, his development can then proceed comfortably and he will no longer be in danger of finding himself in a "squeeze" which gradually becomes more and more unbearable. At the same time, as Black successfully avoids a constricted position, he also solves satisfactorily the puzzling riddle of developing his "problem-child" Queen Bishop in a satisfactory manner.

In each of the following games, therefore, the criteria of Black's success are that he frees his position by simplifying, and that his Queen Bishop is satisfactorily mobilized. When Black achieves these objectives, he has solved his opening problem conclusively and can look forward to the middle game with complete confidence in his prospects.

CHAPTER 14

LASKER'S DEFENSE

I

Simplification Leads to Freedom

Anyone who has had trouble defending against the Queen's Gambit—and who hasn't?—will marvel at the ease with which Black obtains an excellent game.

As we have emphasized, the keynote of Lasker's Defense is *simplification*. Each exchange makes Black's position less burdensome; the exchange of center Pawns permits the effective development of his "problem" Bishop; before long, Black has real threats and works up a devastating initiative.

QUEEN'S GAMBIT DECLINED
ARGENTINE CHAMPIONSHIP, 1948

WHITE	BLACK
Martinez	*C. Guimard*
1 P—Q4	P—Q4
2 P—QB4	P—K3

Black plays 2 . . . P—K3 because he must fight for control of the center, by supporting his Queen Pawn. The Alekhine-Prat game (page 199) forcibly illustrates the consequences of omitting this move, 2 . . . P—K3. Black's pieces are banished from the center because he lacks a center Pawn to assure him a foothold in that vital area.

After 2 . . . P—K3, as played here, Black is assured of that foothold which is so valuable to him; should White at any time play PxP, Black replies . . . PxP and in this way retains control of his K5. Thus White's expansion in the center by P—K4 is restrained and there is no likelihood that Black can be smashed by a concerted advance of the White Pawns.

                3   N—QB3   N—KB3

Each of these Knight moves has a bearing, as you see, on the control of the vital center square known as K4 from White's side of the board, and K5 from Black's side of the board.

                4   B—N5   . . . .

DIAGRAM 108

(after 4 B—N5)
The fight for control of the
center is in full swing.

White develops another piece, and this move too has a bearing on control of the vital center square K4 (Black's K5). For Black's Knight on KB3 is now pinned,* and hence it does not play a role any longer in the struggle for control of the center.

                4   . . . .   B—K2

A useful move. It develops another Black piece, and it prepares for castling. Even more important is the fact that it releases the pin on the King Knight, so that this piece is again able to take part in the struggle for control of the center.

                5   N—B3   Castles

* For the pin, see *Winning Chess*, p. 7.

Note that the move 5 . . . PxP *?*, always attractive to inexperienced players, would not win a Pawn. Worse yet, the capture would be quite bad.

In reply to 5 . . . PxP White simply plays 6 P—K4, monopolizing the center and immediately regaining the Pawn with the developing move 7 BxP. So we see that for the time being at least, Black is well advised to stick to his basic plan of maintaining a Pawn at Q4.

6   P—K3

DIAGRAM 109

(after 6 P—K3)
White's formation leads to aggressiveness—Black's, to passivity.

White's position in the center is more modest than in the Alekhine-Prat game (page 199), but he can nevertheless be well satisfied with his position.

The situation now arrived at is seen very frequently in modern play. It leads generally to a type of game which is exceedingly difficult for Black because of his cramped position. His worst problem is that of developing the Queen Bishop, which is hemmed in by the Black King Pawn. (White's Queen Bishop, on the other hand, is aggressively posted at KN5.)

There are other troublesome aspects to Black's game. His Queen has no good squares. (White's Queen can play to QB2 or QN3 or—after B—Q3—to K2.)

Black's King Bishop fulfills a purely defensive function on K2, breaking the force of the original pin on the Knight at KB3. (White's King Bishop, on the other hand, will have a fine post at Q3, trained on the castled position of Black's King.)

Even Black's Queen Knight is a problem. If played to QB3, it blocks Black's chances of . . . P—B4—a move that is needed to create capturing possibilities with resulting open files for the Rooks. The dilemma here is that . . . N—QB3 looks natural but closes important files to the Black Rooks; while . . . QN—Q2 leaves the possibility of . . . P—B4 open but leads to a cramped position.

What Black needs, then, is a defense which banishes all or most of these difficulties, and also neutralizes some of the favorable factors at White's disposal.

We need a defense which results in the exchange of some pieces, so that Black can get elbow room for his remaining forces, while at the same time White's initiative loses some of its sting.

(*We return now to the position of Diagram 109.*)

6 . . . .   P—KR3

Feeling out White's intentions. Thus if 7 BxN, BxB and Black's position has become somewhat freer and his possession of two Bishops against a Bishop and Knight gives him good prospects for the later play.

The move . . . P—KR3, moreover, has potential uses: it creates an escape square for the Black Monarch which may become necessary during the future course of the game; it may also serve as a prop for a later King-side attack, with . . . P—KN4. As . . . P—KR3 can be played here without loss of time (White must move a developed piece for the second time), Black gets it in at no cost to himself.

7 B—R4   . . . .

After 7 B—B4 Black continues 7 . . . P—B4 with a satisfactory position (he will proceed with . . . N—B3 and then

. . . P—QN3 and . . . B—N2, solving the problem of the Queen Bishop).

7 . . . .   N—K5 !

This is the key move of Lasker's Defense, the line of play which we recommend for Black. It has the virtue of eliminating a great number of inordinately difficult alternative variations, and narrowing the play down to a very small number of lines in all of which White must allow at least one exchange with consequent easing of Black's constricted position.

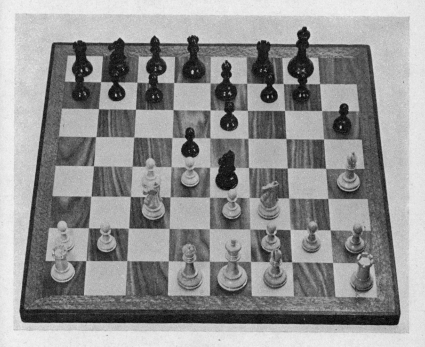

Figure 11

The key to LASKER'S DEFENSE lies in the early . . . N—K5 ! which gives Black a chance to simplify and thus obtain a freedom which is beyond his grasp in most variations of the QUEEN'S GAMBIT DECLINED.

Whether he likes it or not, White must now agree to some simplifying exchange. Here are some of the possibilities:

I. 8 B—N3, NxN; 9 PxN, P—QB4 and Black develops comfortably with . . . N—B3 and . . . P—QN3 and . . . B—N2.

II. 8 NxN, PxN; 9 BxB, QxB; 10 N—Q2, P—K4 ! This line of play will be discussed in more detail later on.

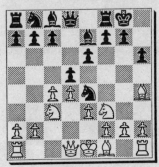

DIAGRAM 110

(after 7 . . . N—K5 !)
Black seeks freedom through
simplifying.

8   BxB   QxB

Black's position has visibly improved. His King Knight has an aggressive position at K5. His Queen is well situated at K2. White has had to part with a well-posted Bishop for Black's rather passive King Bishop.

Black is even a bit ahead in development! Both players have developed two pieces, but Black is castled, while White's King is still in the center. True, Black still has to solve the problem of his Queen Bishop.

White has several possible systems of development at his disposal, but Black can look forward to any of them with quiet confidence.

Thus, if 9 B—Q3, NxN; 10 PxN, PxP !; 11 BxP, P—QN3 ! followed by . . . B—N2 giving the Black Bishop a beautiful long diagonal. Rarely is Black lucky enough to find such a

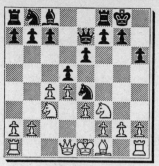

DIAGRAM 111

(after 8 . . . QxB)
Black's position has become
more comfortable.

happy solution for his "problem child" in this opening! Giving up *Pawn* control of the center is unobjectionable when it is superseded by *Bishop* control of the center.

If 9 Q—B2, NxN; 10 QxN, P—QB3 and eventually Black will develop his Bishop satisfactorily.

If 9 NxN, PxN; 10 N—Q2 and now Black momentarily ignores his attacked Pawn, playing 10 . . . P—K4 ! (It would be a mistake for White to reply 11 NxP because of 11 . . . PxP; 12 QxP ? ?, R—Q1 ! and White's Knight is lost.) To recapitulate: after 9 NxN, PxN; 10 N—Q2, P—K4 ! the continuation might be 11 P—Q5, B—B4 (beautiful development for the Bishop!); 12 Q—B2, N—Q2 !; * 13 B—K2, B—N3; 14 O—O, P—KB4. Black can follow up with . . . N—B4, giving him a splendid game. All of his opening difficulties have been solved.

(*We return now to the position of Diagram 111.*)

         9   **PxP**   . . . .

Obviously this cannot be answered by 9 . . . PxP ? for then 10 NxP wins a Pawn.

---

* Black does not mind offering a Pawn, as after 13 NxP, BxN; 14 QxB, Q—N5 *ch* he regains the Pawn most advantageously. Double attack. See *Winning Chess*, p. 50.

DIAGRAM 112

(after 9 PxP)
More simplification!

9 . . . .   NxN

This saves the Pawn—and of course Black is glad to simplify
some more.

10 PxN   PxP

DIAGRAM 113

(after 10 . . . PxP)
Note the open line for Black's
Bishop!

"Suddenly" the problem of Black's Queen Bishop is solved!
The Bishop's diagonal is opened, and such moves as . . . B—
K3 or . . . B—B4 or . . . B—N5 have now become possible.
Note that this favorable turn of events has come about be-

cause of the previous *exchange of Pawns*. Another consequence of this Pawn exchange is that Black has a half-open
King file, so that he can exert pressure on the important square
K5 with his Queen, or in some cases, with a Rook. *Always
study Pawn captures for their effects in opening files and diagonals and thus enhancing the mobility of your pieces.*

Black's basic strategic idea of *simplification* has yielded him
a satisfying measure of freedom. Now his aim is to bring out
his pieces rapidly, fighting for the initiative.

11   Q—N3   . . . .

White attacks the Queen Pawn and at the same time keeps
the Queen Knight Pawn under observation, impeding the development of Black's Bishop.

11   . . . .   R—Q1

11 . . . P—QB3 is inferior, as it takes away the square QB3
from Black's Knight (see Black's 13th move).

11 . . . Q—Q3 is the usual move nowadays, the idea being
to reserve the square Q1 for the Queen Rook.

12   P—B4   PxP

At last Black gives up his *Pawn* control of K5, but he intends
to take counter-measures against the possibility of White's center Pawns becoming too powerful.

13   BxP   N—B3

This takes the sting out of a possible N—K5 by White.

Black's last move (13 . . . N—B3) seems at first sight a
contradiction of what was said in the note to 6 P—K3 (page
145) about the need for not blocking the Queen Bishop Pawn.

The general theory is that the Queen Bishop Pawn must be
played to QB4 *before* the Knight is developed at QB3. If the
Knight is played out first, the opportunity for Pawn exchanges
is lost and the Rooks will have no open files on which to operate. (See the game Alekhine-Prat—page 199—on this point.)

DIAGRAM 114

(after 13 . . . N—B3)
The Knight is developed with
gain of time.

In the present case, however, Black's Rooks can be placed
usefully on the King file and Queen file. Hence Black has no
great interest in opening the Queen Bishop file for his Rooks.

But 13 . . . N—B3 has many valuable aspects. As we have
observed, it takes the sting out of White's contemplated N—
K5. It also threatens 14 . . . N—R4, with the possible sequel
15 Q—B3, NxB; 16 QxN, B—K3 (splendid development of the
Bishop with gain of time); 17 Q—B3, B—Q4 and Black has a
highly effective Bishop against a mediocre Knight. Most players would give their eye-teeth for as good a position as this
against the Queen's Gambit!

Still another virtue of 13 . . . N—B3 is that it induces
White to relax his pressure against the Queen Knight Pawn, so
that Black can at last develop his Bishop.

(*We return now to the position of Diagram 114.*)

14   Q—B3   . . . .

Forestalling a possible . . . N—R4. But now Black's Bishop
can come out.

14   . . . .   B—N5 !

This is quite in order now, as his Queen Knight Pawn is no
longer under attack.

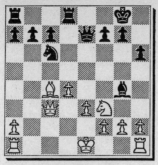

DIAGRAM 115

(after 14 . . . B—N5 *!*)
Black's "problem" Bishop is
developed!

The initiative has slipped from White's hands; he is afraid to
castle, for after 15 Castles (K), BxN; 16 PxB the rampart of
protective Pawns in front of the castled King is broken up and
Black has good attacking chances with . . . R—Q3 in con-
junction with . . . Q—N4 *ch* or . . . Q—R5. Such exposed situations are particularly dangerous for inexperienced players.

(*We return now to the position of Diagram 115.*)

15   B—K2   . . . .

White thinks he is playing safe, but he cannot avoid complications.

15   . . . .   BxN *!*
16   PxB   . . . .

He dismisses 16 BxB because of 16 . . . NxP *!* (the King
Pawn is pinned); 17 BxP, QR—N1; 18 B—R6, Q—B3 (threat-
ening a catastrophe for White by 19 . . . N—B6 *ch* or 19
. . . N—B7 *ch* *); 19 PxN, QxB and the exposed position of
White's King is bound to be fatal.

16   . . . .   R—Q3
17   KR—N1   . . . .

* Double attack, See *Winning Chess*, p. 50.

White wants to attack on the open King Knight file. His threat is 18 P—Q5 (attacking the Knight and menacing QxP mate), N—K4; 19 P—B4 and the pinned Knight is lost, for if 19 N—N3; 20 P—B5, N—K4; 21 P—B4.*

17 . . . .   NxP *! !*

A retort as beautiful as it is unexpected.

DIAGRAM 116

(after 17 . . . NxP *!!*)
Sacrifice or investment?!

18 R—Q1   . . . .

If 18 PxN, R—K1; 19 Q—K3, R—K3 winning the pinned Bishop!

18 . . . .   N—K3

The Knight retreats unharmed and guards against the threatened mate at Black's KN2.

19 P—B4   . . . .

This time his threat is 20 P—B5, N—N4 (the only Knight move which prevents the mate); 21 P—KR4 again winning the fatally pinned Knight.

* For this pinning motif (which recurs in the notes to White's 18th and 19th moves), see *Winning Chess,* p. 7.

19	. . . .	RxR *ch*
20	BxR	R—Q1 *!*

It would seem that he overlooks White's threat.

21	P—B5	. . . .

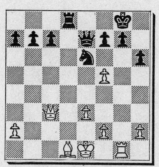

DIAGRAM 117

(after 21 P—B5)
White sees a glimmer of hope.

White looks forward to 21 . . . N—N4; 22 P—KR4 winning a piece because of the mating threat against Black's KN2.

21	. . . .	Q—Q3 *!*

Nicely played. White has no time for 22 PxN *? ?* because of the reply 22 . . . QxB mate!

White cannot play 22 Q—R1 (guarding the Bishop and still maintaining his threat against Black's KN2) because of 22 . . . Q—Q7 *ch* winning a piece with easy victory in sight.

22 Q—B2 guards the Bishop but renounces the mating threat.

22 B—B3 allows 22 . . . N—N4 *!* as a valid reply because of the threatened 23 . . . NxB *ch* followed by . . . NxR.

22 B—B2 or 22 B—N3 allows 22 . . . N—N4 when 23 P—KR4 *?* can be answered by 23 . . . N—B6 *ch* forking King and Rook.

22 B—N4 is meaningless because it blocks the open King Knight file, putting an end to the mate threat.

On 22 B—K2 Black can play 22 . . . QxP attacking the White Rook. Play might continue 23 R—N4 (keeping the mate threat alive), N—N4; 24 P—B4, Q—R8 *ch;* 25 B—B1,* N—B6 *ch;* 26 K—B2, R—Q7 *ch;* 27 K—N3, Q—N8 *ch;* 28 KxN, QxB *ch;* 29 K—K4, Q—R8 *ch* and mate follows.

22   B—R5   QxP

DIAGRAM 118

(after 22 . . . QxP)
White's attack is more bark
than bite.

23   BxP *ch*   . . . .

Desperation. He hopes for 23 . . . KxB, giving him time to play 24 PxN *ch* with threats against Black's King.

23   . . . .   K—R1 *!*

Now White still doesn't have time to capture the Knight: 24 PxN ? ?, QxR *ch;* 25 K—K2, Q—Q8 mate!

24   R—B1   N—N4

If now 25 B—B4, N—B6 *ch;* 26 K—K2, Q—R4 *!* and White is helpless against the terrible double check 27 . . . N—

* 25 K—B2 ? ? allows the fork 25 . . . N—K5 *ch* winning the Queen. See *Winning Chess,* p. 29.

N8 *ch.* If for example 27 B—B7, N—N8 *dbl ch;* 28 K—K1 and
Black can mate in three different ways! If 27 B—Q3 then 27
. . . N—K4 *dis ch* wins a piece.

25   Q—B4   . . . .

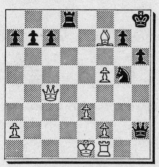

DIAGRAM 119

(after 25 Q—B4)
Black's next move is crushing.

25 . . . .   Q—Q3 *!*
      Resigns

The threat of 26 . . . Q—Q8 mate or 26 . . . Q—Q7 mate
is too much for him.

If White moves the Queen to stop mate, the Bishop is lost.

**In this game we have seen how Black solves his major problems:
how to develop his pieces; how to simplify in order to free his constricted position; how to develop his "problem child" the Queen
Bishop; how to get his Rooks into active play. The overall effect of
these measures has been very satisfactory for Black.**

CHAPTER 15

LASKER'S DEFENSE

II

Normal Position for Black

From the ease with which Black equalized and soon obtained the initiative in Chapter 14, you can readily understand why authorities on opening play consider Lasker's Defense the greatest menace to White's hope of acquiring a lasting initiative with 1 P—Q4.

The key to Black's success, we must emphasize again and again, lies in purposeful reliance on *simplification through early exchanges,* with resulting freedom for his "problem" Bishop. Study the functions of the King Bishop, King Knight, Queen Pawn and King Pawn in this chapter to perfect your exchanging technique. In this way you will be able to achieve freedom at a remarkably early stage when defending against the Queen's Gambit.

Bear in mind that obtaining freedom so quickly *is a great success in itself.* It is not a guarantee of victory, and should not breed over-confidence. But that freedom, once atttained, is a great aid to middle game planning; your hands are not tied by the kind of pervasive positional pressure which White exercises so frequently in the Queen's Gambit Declined.

The Black Pawns

The KING ROOK PAWN plays to KR3 in the opening, compelling White to make up his mind about the attacked Queen Bishop at KN5 (the usual reaction is B—KR4) and also creating a loophole for Black's King at KR2 after Black castles.

The KING KNIGHT PAWN remains at KN2.

The KING BISHOP PAWN remains at KB2, except that in those cases where White exchanges Knights on his K4 (after . . . N—K5) and Black replies . . . PxN, he will generally support the advanced King Pawn with . . . P—KB4. (See Martinez-Guimard, note to Black's eighth move.)

The KING PAWN plays to K3 in the opening. Later on in the game White usually exchanges Pawns in the center (BPxQP), whereupon Black recaptures with his King Pawn (. . . KPxQP) opening up the diagonal for his Queen Bishop. Where White exchanges Knights on his K4 (see above), Black generally frees himself by playing . . . P—K4 later on. In the variations where Black plays . . . QPxBP (Scheltinga-Grau) to open the fianchetto diagonal for his Queen Bishop, he will often play . . . P—K4 in the early middle game. Wherever . . . P—K4 is feasible, it has a marked emancipating effect on Black's position.

The QUEEN PAWN is removed by exchange early in the game. Either White plays BPxQP (as in Martinez-Guimard); or Black plays . . . QPxBP (as in Scheltinga-Grau) to open the fianchetto diagonal for his Queen Bishop; or else, where the Knights are exchanged on White's K4 (this has been described previously), Black's Queen Pawn reaches K5 by means of . . . QPxN.

The QUEEN BISHOP PAWN remains on QB2 in most variations. There are two cases in which it advances to QB4: (a) after . . . N—QB3—K2 (Eliskases-Gruenfeld); (b) after . . . QPxBP and the fianchetto of Black's Queen Bishop (Scheltinga-Grau). The purpose of this advance of the Queen Bishop Pawn is of course to give a Black Rook maneuvering scope on the Queen Bishop file.

The QUEEN KNIGHT PAWN stays on QN2, except in the variation in which Black fianchettoes his Queen Bishop (Scheltinga-Grau), when . . . P—QN3 is played to prepare for the Bishop's development.

The QUEEN ROOK PAWN generally remains on QR2.

The Black Pieces

The KING KNIGHT goes to KB3 and then to K5—this is the thematic simplifying move which characterizes the whole defense.

The QUEEN KNIGHT goes to QB3 in most variations, this being one of the few instances in which a satisfactory development may be achieved in a Queen Pawn opening with the Knight blocking the Queen Bishop Pawn. Later on it often plays to K2 and Q4, where it is effectively posted in the center. The Queen Knight goes to Q2, however, in those variations in which the Queen Bishop is fianchettoed (this is illustrated in Scheltinga-Grau).

The KING BISHOP plays to K2 and is soon exchanged for White's Queen Bishop by means of the thematic simplifying maneuver . . . N—K5. A short history but a very satisfying one for Black.

The QUEEN BISHOP, generally a severe problem for Black in the Queen's Gambit Declined, offers no trouble here. In the variations in which White exchanges Pawns in the center (BPxQP) Black recaptures with the King Pawn, and is then in a position to develop the Queen Bishop handsomely (. . . B—KN5). Once the Bishop goes to KN5, it is generally exchanged for White's King Knight on White's KB3. This is a useful feature of Black's simplifying strategy, and has a weakening effect on White's Pawn structure. The open King Knight file which White obtains from this exchange is of little use to him. In the variations in which Black exchanges Pawns in the center (. . . QPxQBP), he thereby opens up the fianchetto diagonal for his Queen Bishop, whereupon . . . P—QN3 and . . . B—N2 is in order. In this case, too, the Bishop has a fine diagonal, bearing down very strongly on the center squares.

The KING ROOK goes to KB1 when Black castles. Later on the Rook may play to K1 when the King file is opened as a result of Pawn exchanges in the center (BPxQP as in Martinez-Guimard). When Black exchanges Pawns in the center (. . .

Figure 12

*The typical Pawn formation in the main line of LASKER'S DE-
FENSE. The exchange of Pawns has made it possible for Black to
develop his Queen Bishop effectively.*

QPxBP as in Scheltinga-Grau) the King Rook may be usefully
deployed at Q1 or even at QB1.

The QUEEN ROOK's development is likewise determined by
the nature of Black's Pawn position. Thus after . . . QPxBP
(Scheltinga-Grau) Black's Queen Rook stays at QR1 to guard
the Queen Rook Pawn. In Martinez-Guimard a Black Rook
goes to Q1 to operate on the half-open Queen file. The same
development is seen in Bonham-Isles and Eliskases-Gruenfeld.
So that the placement of one Black Rook at Q1 and the other at
K1 may be taken as fairly standard in this variation, each Rook
being stationed on a half-open file.

The QUEEN plays to K2 as a result of the early exchange of Bishops at Black's K2. This is an ideal position for the Queen, supporting action in the center (eventual . . . P—K4 or pressure on K5); threatening . . . Q—N5 *ch* in some cases; playing to KB3 with attack on White's doubled King Bishop Pawn. Another useful consequence of the Black Queen's position at K2 is that Black's Rooks are given an early opportunity to occupy the center files. This effective functioning of Black's Queen is in contrast to many variations of the Queen's Gambit Declined in which this piece has very little scope.

Review: Salient objectives for Black

(1) Exchanges of King Bishop, King Knight and Queen Pawn basic to Black's plan.

(2) Open diagonal must be created for "problem" Queen Bishop.

(3) Queen has effective pivot square at K2—can go to KB3 or Q3.

(4) Queen Knight often goes to QB3—contrary to general rule.

(5) Rooks occupy half-open files—either at K1 and Q1, or Q1 and QB1.

CHAPTER 16

LASKER'S DEFENSE

III

A Fatal Dilemma for White

Playing along the same lines as in Chapter 14, Black solves the difficulties of the opening very quickly. He has good possibilities of development for all his pieces, including the "problem" Bishop. And so, as in Chapter 14, he enters the middle game with excellent prospects and no worries.

But White has a serious psychological difficulty: should he reconcile himself to the fact that Black has perfect equality and merely play to maintain the status quo? Should he refuse to content himself with this puny result, and insist on White's birthright—the initiative?

Black, on the other hand, dispenses with all soul-searching. He has equality, which to Black is always a distinct qualitative success. In effect he tells White: "Theory holds that you are supposed to have an opening advantage. I see no evidence for it in this game, but if you want to prove your theory, go ahead. I'm all set to take whatever punishment you can hand out, and I'm satisfied that I can hit back harder." We submit that Black has a good case!

QUEEN'S GAMBIT DECLINED

BRITISH CHAMPIONSHIP, 1950

WHITE	BLACK
R. W. Bonham	E. A. Isles
1 P—Q4	P—Q4
2 P—QB4	P—K3

3	N—QB3	N—KB3
4	B—N5	B—K2
5	P—K3	Castles
6	N—B3	P—KR3
7	B—R4	N—K5
8	BxB	QxB
9	PxP	NxN
10	PxN	PxP
11	Q—N3	R—Q1
12	P—B4	PxP
13	BxP	N—B3
14	Q—B3	B—N5

DIAGRAM 120

(after 14 . . . B—N5)
Again Black has an exception-
ally satisfactory development.

Thus far the play has been identical with that of the previous game. Black has simplified the position, obtained good
lines of development for his pieces, and again White is faced
with the problem of allowing . . . BxN or evading the exchange by N—Q2.

15	Castles(K)	BxN
16	PxB	Q—B3

White has allowed . . . BxN, and the problems which now
confront both players are extremely interesting.

DIAGRAM 121

(after 16 . . . Q—B3)
Black has a very promising
position for the middle game.

The open King Knight file beckons to White as a source of
attacking possibilities. He intends to tuck his King away in the
corner and then double his Rooks on the King Knight file.
Black is not particularly worried about this, as he will simply
reply . . . P—KN3 at the proper moment and be quite safe.
Another point is that if White concentrates his Rooks on the
King Knight file, he will be neglecting the center and Queen-
side.

At first sight White's Pawn cluster in the center looks powerful, but actually these Pawns are awkward to manipulate. If,
for example, White now answers the threat of . . . QxBP
with 17 P—B4, we find that his King Bishop Pawn, King Pawn
and Queen Pawn are immobilized for quite a while to come.

Nor can White play 17 P—K4, for then his Queen Pawn
would be lost. But even when P—K4 is possible, it would be
of dubious value, for it would allow some such move as . . .
Q—B5 or (later on) . . . N—KB5. The point involved here is
that White's KB4 is a black square and therefore cannot be
guarded by his Bishop. Consequently this square can be occupied very effectively by Black's pieces in the event that White's
King Pawn relaxes its watch over this square. This is exactly
what happens later on.

Again we have the same picture as in the previous game. Black, *being content with equality,* solves his problem rather easily and has little to worry about. White, having the traditional "advantage of the first move," feels obligated to strive for a win. Since the position now arrived at, does not justify this ambition, White is in a frustrated mood which may easily lead him to try for more than the position justifies.

(*We return now to the position of Diagram 121.*)

17　B—K2　　　. . . .

As White does not want to commit himself with P—B4, he must degrade the Bishop to this purely defensive function.

DIAGRAM 122

(after 17 B—K2)
White must fight desperately
for the initiative.

17　. . . .　　　R—Q2

Black wants to be able to move his Knight. Before he can do so, he must guard the Queen Bishop Pawn; hence the Rook move.

18　K—R1　　　. . . .

He prepares to place his Rooks on the King Knight file. There was still time to discard this illogical plan, substituting Queen-side play (18 QR—N1).

18	. . . .	N—K2
19	R—KN1	N—Q4

Now the Knight is more aggressively posted in the center. An eventual P—K4 can be countered effectively by . . . N—B5.

20	Q—N3	Q—QN3

DIAGRAM 123

(after 20 . . . Q—QN3)
Black confronts his opponent
with a difficult decision.

White should now exchange Queens, with a draw as the likely outcome—although White's Pawn position would be inferior. This would be a very satisfactory windup as far as the student is concerned, our objective being to find a defense that eliminates the "ills that flesh is heir to" on the Black side of the Queen's Gambit Declined.

But White wants to get more and ends up in defeat.

21	Q—B2	Q—K3
22	B—B4	Q—KB3

Here again White can simplify with 23 BxN, RxB. But this time Black would have an unmistakable edge: White's attack is gone, his King Bishop Pawn and Queen Rook Pawn require attention; his King must not be deserted, as the broken-up state of his King-side Pawns may prove dangerous for him;

DIAGRAM 124

(after 22 . . . Q—KB3)
Again White must make a difficult decision.

Black's Queen-side majority of three Pawns to two can be
transformed into a passed Pawn after due preparation, tying
White's forces down to defensive work.

Again it must be emphasized that White is burdened with
decisions which are extremely troubling from a psychological
point of view: nothing is more harassing in chess than trying
to attain a goal with clearly inadequate means. Black, on the
other hand, has an easy time of it: he wants at least equality,
and retains it effortlessly and without risk.

23	Q—K4	P—B3
24	R—N3	P—KN3
25	QR—KN1	. . . .

Threatening to win the Queen and some Pawns, in return
for two Rooks, by 26 RxP *ch*, PxR; 27 RxP *ch* etc. But Black's
obvious reply parries the threat (*see Diagram 125*):

25	. . . .	K—N2
26	Q—N4	R(Q2)—Q1
27	P—K4?	. . . .

As forecast in the note to Black's 16th move, White finally
weakens his position with this impulsive advance.

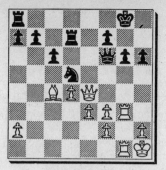

DIAGRAM 125

(after 25 QR—KN1)
Black is threatened with the
loss of his Queen.

27 P—B4 was the right move. The text allows Black to
decide the game with a smart finish.

27 . . . . P—KR4 !

DIAGRAM 126

(after 27 . . . P—KR4 !)
The turning point: Black has
a winning attack.

If White declines the unexpected offer of a Pawn, his position is hopeless just the same: for example 28 Q—N5, N—N3
and Black simultaneously attacks the Bishop and the Queen

Pawn; or 28 Q—R3, N—B5; 29 Q—B1, RxP and Black wins easily.

(We return now to the position of Diagram 126.)

28   QxRP   . . . .

The Pawn win is made possible by the fact that Black's King Knight Pawn is pinned. But White's happiness is of short duration.

28   . . . .   N—B5

Now the White Queen is really attacked and must move.

DIAGRAM 127

(after 28 . . . N—B5)
An important gain of time for
Black.

White has no good continuation. If 29 Q—KN5, QxQ; 30 RxQ, N—R6 winning the exchange.* If 29 Q—K5, RxP; 30 QxQ *ch*, KxQ and Black has an easily won game: open files, three Pawns to one on the Queen-side, a dominating post for his Knight.

(We return now to the position of Diagram 127.)

29   Q—QB5   R—R1

With the brutal threat of 30 . . . RxP *ch!*, 31 KxR, Q—R5 *ch* and mate next move.

* Double attack. See *Winning Chess*, p. 50.

This fearsome menace highlights the dangers created for White by the breakup of the Pawn position resulting from 15 . . . BxN.

Note that if 30 Q—K5 or 30 Q—KN5, Black forces mate with 30 . . . RxP *ch !;* 31 KxR, R—R1 *ch* etc.

30 P—KR3 leads to the same finish as actually occurs in the game.

30   **B—B1**   **R—R4**

Gaining time to double the Rooks.

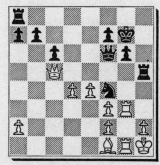

DIAGRAM 128

(after 30 . . . R—R4)
Black will triumph on the
King Rook file.

If now 31 R—N5, QR—R1 threatening mate on the move. White is then lost. Thus if 32 RxR, RxR attacking the Queen and also threatening 33 . . . RxP *ch !;* 34 KxR, Q—R5 *ch* and mate next move.

Or if 31 R—N5, QR—R1; 32 P—KR3, RxP *ch !;* 33 BxR, RxB mate!

(*We return now to the position of Diagram 128.*)

31   **Q—B3**   **QR—R1**

Threatening mate on the move.

32   **P—KR3**   **Q—R5 !!**

33   P—Q5 *dis ch*   K—B1
     Resigns

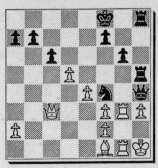

DIAGRAM 129

(after 33 . . . K—B1)
White is helpless against
Black's coming Queen sacri-
fice!

White is helpless, as he must give up his Queen for a Rook
to prevent mate.

Thus if 34 K—R2, QxP *ch ! !;* 35 BxQ, RxB *ch;* 36 RxR, RxR
mate! If 34 R(N1)—N2, QxP *ch ! !;* 35 RxQ, RxR *ch;* 36 R—R2,
RxR *ch;* 37 K—N1, R—R8 mate!

As in the Martinez-Guimard game, p. 143, Black quickly freed
his position, developed his pieces favorably and obtained a decisive attack.

But even more important, as we have emphasized, is the psychological difficulty in which White finds himself because of the un-
canny rapidity with which Black obtains a promising position for
the middle game.

CHAPTER 17

LASKER'S DEFENSE

IV

Battleground of Conflicting Theories

If you have studied the last three chapters attentively, you have realized that Lasker's Defense is a crucial attempt to refute the theory that the first move gives White an advantage.

Opening authorities have therefore busied themselves with this defense, striving with might and main to refute it. One such attempt is seen in White's 15 N—Q2, essayed by Eliskases in the following game.

As the course of the play indicates, Black has no trouble at all in maintaining equality, and, in fact, as we show in our notes, he missed at least one good winning chance.

However, the ease with which Black obtains a draw is in itself a qualitative success. *The onus of winning is on White!* Black's problem is to find a defense which allows him to enter the middle game without disadvantage, and this is the problem which Lasker's Defense solves to perfection.

QUEEN'S GAMBIT DECLINED
UJPEST, 1934

WHITE	BLACK
E. Eliskases	E. Gruenfeld
1 P—Q4	N—KB3
2 P—QB4	P—K3
3 N—QB3	P—Q4
4 B—N5	B—K2

5	P—K3	Castles
6	N—B3	P—KR3
7	B—R4	N—K5
8	BxB	QxB
9	PxP	NxN
10	PxN	PxP
11	Q—N3	. . . .

DIAGRAM 130

(after 11 Q—N3)
Black chooses a different
method of guarding his Queen
Pawn.

So far the game has proceeded along the same lines as in
Chapters 14 and 16.

Black can consider himself fairly out of the opening difficulties. His position is no longer constricted, his Bishop has a
clear path for development, his Rooks can be usefully posted
at Q1 and K1 in due course.

| 11 | . . . . | Q—Q3 |

Guimard, you will recall, protected the Queen Pawn by 11
. . . R—Q1. The kind of position reached is much the same.

| 12 | P—B4 | PxP |
| 13 | BxP | N—B3 |

DIAGRAM 131

(after 13 . . . N—B3)
White is reluctant to allow
the simplifying . . . N—R4.

You know from Chapters 14 and 16, that this move is generally considered "unscientific" in Queen Pawn games when it blocks the Queen Bishop Pawn and consequently leaves little scope for the Rooks. But, as we saw in that game, Black has ample play for his Rooks on the King file and Queen file.

14   Q—B3   . . . .

White wastes a move in order to banish the annoying possibility of . . . N—R4, whereby Black would bring about further simplification of the position. But the Queen move permits the immediate development of Black's Bishop.

14 . . . .   B—N5
15   N—Q2   . . . .

Here we definitely part company with the two previous games. White retreats his Knight to avoid . . . BxN, breaking up his Pawn position on the King-side. 15 N—Q2 is certainly the safe course, but it is interesting to pause to reflect on the general trend of the game. 13 . . . N—B3 was a developing move which involved a threat requiring a non-developing reply by White. 14 . . . B—N5, again, was a developing move which involved a threat and induced White to make a non-developing reply.

DIAGRAM 132

(after 15 N—Q2)
White has avoided the possibility of . . . BxN.

One can safely conclude that Black's situation is very satisfactory, and that he has nothing to fear.

15	. . . .	QR—Q1
16	QR—B1	. . . .

Another way is 16 Castles(K), N—K2; 17 KR—B1, P—QN3; 18 N—K4, Q—Q2 with even chances.

16	. . . .	N—K2
17	Castles	. . . .

Now Black can play a move which makes his position quite comfortable. (*See Diagram 133.*)

17	. . . .	P—QB4

If now 18 PxP *?* Black wins a piece with 18 . . . QxN—and not 18 . . . QxBP *? ?* allowing 19 BxP *ch* winning the Queen.*

18	N—K4	. . . .

* Discovered attack. See *Winning Chess,* p. 67.

DIAGRAM 133

(after 17 Castles)
Black takes advantage of the
fact that the Queen Pawn is
pinned.

At first sight this seems to win a Pawn because of the attack
on Black's Queen and the double attack on his Queen Bishop
Pawn.

DIAGRAM 134

(after 18 N—K4)
What is Black's strongest continuation?

18 . . . .   PxP

Avoiding a loss of material because of the counterattack on
White's Queen.

A more aggressive alternative is 18 . . . Q—KN3 attacking the Knight. In that case 19 NxP? is bad because of 19 . . . B—R6 * threatening mate. After the compulsory reply 20 P—N3 Black wins the exchange by 20 . . . BxR, and with the material advantage of Rook for Bishop and Pawn, should win the game.

19	NxQ	PxQ
20	NxNP	R—Q2

DIAGRAM 135

(after 20 . . . R—Q2)
Where should the Knight retreat?

21	N—R5	. . . .

If instead 21 N—B5, R—B2; 22 RxP! (the only way to prevent loss of a piece), RxN!; 23 BxP ch!,** KxB; 24 RxR and White has Rook and two Pawns against Bishop and Knight. As this is a rough material equivalent, the outcome should be a draw.

21	. . . .	R—B2
22	P—B3	. . . .

White plays safe. If 22 RxP?, KR—B1; 23 KR—B1 (threatening the discovered attack 24 BxP ch), B—K3! reinforcing

* The pin. See *Winning Chess*, p. 7.
** Discovered attack. See *Winning Chess*, p. 67.

the pin * and preparing to win material by 24 . . . R—B4 !
Once the protective Knight is forced away from QR5, White
will suffer a decisive loss of material.

Realizing this, White wisely refuses to subject himself to the
dangerous pin.

22	. . . .	B—K3
23	BxB	PxB

The game was abandoned as a draw a few moves later. At
no time was Black in difficulties, and it may well be that he
missed good winning chances by not playing the enterprising
18 . . . Q—KN3.

The important aspect of this game, as pointed out in the intro-
duction, is that Black enters the middle game with excellent prospects. This represents a defeat for White's attempt to question the
adequacy of the defense.

* For the pin, see *Winning Chess*, p. 7.

CHAPTER 18

LASKER'S DEFENSE

V

White's Last Attempt at Refutation

IN THIS chapter we deal with White's last attempt to refute the Lasker Defense. The idea is at first sight convincing: in the games so far studied, White exchanges Pawns in the center at a fairly early stage. The consequence of this exchange (see, for example, Diagram 120) is that Black's "problem" Bishop obtains a beautiful diagonal for development. Thus Black's greatest middle game difficulty is at once disposed of.

Hence White reasons: if the exchange of center Pawns emancipates Black's "problem" Bishop, let's not exchange Pawns! Then Black should have the characteristic Queen's Gambit Declined trouble in developing the "problem" Bishop effectively.

True, Black can create a different diagonal for the "problem" Bishop (see Diagram 137). But to do it, he must give up his Pawn control of the center. This exposes him, theoretically, at least, to the danger of being completely overrun in the center.* But, with careful play—we see this admirably managed in the following game—Black maintains control of the center even after surrendering it! And the beauty of the whole process is that this control is established by none other than the problem Bishop!

The situation shown in Diagram 136 is already familiar to us from the earlier games. Black's policy, as we know, is to bring

---

* For an impressive object lesson on the consequences of surrendering the center, see Alekhine-Prat (Chapter 20).

about several exchanges so that White's somewhat greater freedom can be neutralized.

QUEEN'S GAMBIT DECLINED
BUENOS AIRES, 1939

	WHITE	BLACK
	T. van Scheltinga	*R. Grau*
1	P—Q4	P—Q4
2	P—QB4	P—K3
3	N—QB3	N—KB3
4	B—N5	B—K2
5	P—K3	Castles
6	N—B3	P—KR3
7	B—R4	N—K5
8	BxB	QxB

DIAGRAM 136

(after 8 . . . QxB)
White tries a new tack.

Above all, Black must concentrate on the problem of developing his remaining Bishop.

9   Q—B2   . . . .

White tries a new tack. We know from the earlier games that Black has nothing to fear from 9 PxP, NxN; 10 PxN, PxP— or 9 NxN, PxN; 10 N—Q2, P—K4 *!*

9	. . . .	NxN
10	QxN	PxP !

Giving up control of the center, but the situation here is quite different from the one that prevails in the Alekhine-Prat game (Chapter 20), in which Black surrenders the center with catastrophic results.

Black intends to develop his Bishop in fianchetto (at N2), when it will strike powerfully along the long diagonal.

DIAGRAM 137

(after 10 . . . PxP !)
Black opens up a diagonal for
his "problem" Bishop.

11	BxP	. . . .

Quite natural: he develops a new piece and prepares for castling.

If 11 QxP (intending to exert pressure on the open Queen Bishop file), Black follows up consistently with 11 . . . P—QN3 ! preparing to develop his Bishop on a good diagonal. There might follow 12 R—B1 (strengthening the pressure on the open file), P—QB4 ! (temporarily sacrificing a Pawn); 13 PxP, B—R3 !

Black must always recover his Pawn advantageously, for example:

(*Diagram for Variation*)

DIAGRAM 138

White cannot hold the extra
Pawn.

I. 14 Q—QR4, BxB; 15 KxB, R—B1; 16 P—B6, Q—K1 regaining the Pawn with favorable prospects.

II. 14 Q—QR4, BxB; 15 KxB, R—B1; 16 P—QN4, P—QR4! smashing up White's Queen-side Pawns and regaining the lost Pawn with ease.

III. 14 Q—B3, BxB; 15 KxB, R—B1; 16 P—QN4, P—QR4!; 17 P—QR3, RPxP; 18 RPxP, PxP; 19 PxP, N—R3; 20 P—B6, N—N5 and the double threat of 21 . . . N—R7 (winning the exchange) or 21 . . . RxP gives White a very precarious game.

IV. 14 Q—Q4, BxB; 15 KxB, R—B1; 16 P—QN4, P—QR4! and again Black regains his Pawn on very favorable terms.

It is no wonder that these variations turn out poorly for White: he neglects his development, loses the opportunity to castle—and does not succeed in his materialistic aim of winning the Pawn!

Incidentally, these variations are simpler than they seem at first sight. Their details are less important than the logic behind them: Black has to recover the Pawn favorably because of his considerable lead in development.

After this lengthy but vital digression, we return to the course of the actual game after 11 BxP from the following position:

DIAGRAM 139

(after 11 BxP)
Black has surmounted the first crisis.

| 11 | . . . . | P—QN3 ! |

Black will play . . . B—N2, solving the problem of how to develop his "problem child."

| 12 | Castles(K) | B—N2 |
| 13 | B—K2 | . . . . |

Else a possible . . . BxN might lead to a nasty weakening of the White King's position.

White is prepared to answer 13 . . . BxN ? with 14 BxB with a positionally won game because of the powerful position of the White Bishop on the long diagonal.

But of course Black has no intention of parting with his precious Bishop on these unfavorable terms.

Black now requires two moves to complete his development in a logical manner: . . . N—Q2 and . . . P—QB4.

However, he cannot play 13 . . . N—Q2 ? because of the reply 14 QxP.

The argument against 13 . . . P—QB4 is less immediately obvious but equally weighty. After 13 . . . P—QB4 *?*; 14 PxP, PxP; 15 QR—B1 Black's isolated Queen Bishop Pawn is a permanent object of attack because it has no neighboring Pawns to protect it and must therefore be guarded by pieces.

Black finds the right move to brush aside these difficulties:

(*See Diagram 140.*)

13 . . . . R—B1 *!*

Black's troubles are almost over. Now that his Queen Bishop Pawn is protected, . . . N—Q2 has become feasible.

Figure 13

In this variation of LASKER'S DEFENSE, Black completes the freeing process with . . . P—QB4. The advance of this Pawn gives Black pressure on White's center and also frees his position on the Queen Bishop file.

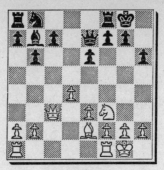

DIAGRAM 140

(after 13 B—K2)
Black must strive for . . . P—
QB4.

. . . P—QB4 is also practicable, as White's PxP can be answered by . . . RxP, avoiding any Pawn weakness and getting
Black's Rook into good play on the open file.

DIAGRAM 141

(after 13 . . . R—B1 !)
Black has made the necessary
preparations for the all-important . . . P—QB4.

14   KR—Q1   P—QB4 !
15   Q—R3   . . . .

White tries to preserve some initiative by pinning * Black's

* For the pin, see *Winning Chess*, p. 7.

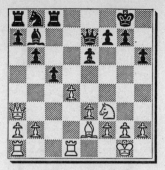

DIAGRAM 142

(after 15 Q—R3)
White relies on a pin for temporary pressure.

Queen Bishop Pawn. (Black naturally cannot play . . . PxP ? ? because of the reply QxQ.)

15 . . . . N—Q2 *!*

Black is doing famously. He has completed his development and his Bishop is posted magnificently.

16 R—Q2 P—K4

DIAGRAM 143

(after 16 . . . P—K4)
Complete emancipation!

Black does not fear the possible reply 17 P—Q5, as he can blockade the passed Queen Pawn with . . . Q—Q3 and maintain a perfectly acceptable position. The Pawn structure would then become locked, with few open lines available to either side. As compensation for White's passed Pawn, Black would have three Pawns to two on the Queen-side; that is to say, he

(Diagram for Variation)

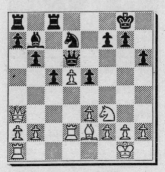

DIAGRAM 144

"Black would have three Pawns to two on the Queen-side."

would have a *potential* passed Pawn himself, based on the advance of his Queen-side Pawns and resulting Pawn exchanges.

(We return now to the position of Diagram 143.)

17	PxBP	NxP
18	QR—Q1	R—B2

Black's position is perfectly satisfactory. His pieces are effectively posted; White has no points of invasion; Black is prepared to double Rooks on the Queen Bishop file, as he need not fear White's QxP in answer to . . . QR—QB1 because of the discovered attack * . . . BxN and wins.

(See Diagram 145.)

19	Q—N4	. . . .

* For discovered attack, see *Winning Chess*, p. 67.

DIAGRAM 145

(after 18 . . . R—B2)
Black prepares to double
Rooks on the Queen Bishop
file.

Having nothing better available, White tries to get his
Queen into more effective play.

19 . . . .   QR—QB1
20 P—KR3   P—N3

Both sides are more or less marking time. Black's position is
somewhat more comfortable, but chances are even.

DIAGRAM 146

(after 20 . . . P—N3)
Black has achieved perfect
equality.

21	Q—N4	K—N2
22	N—R4	. . . .

DIAGRAM 147

(after 22 N—R4)
A temporary flurry: White
threatens to win the Queen!

White now threatens 23 N—B5 *ch* winning the Queen.*
But Black has an easy defense.

22	. . . .	Q—N4
23	QxQ	PxQ
24	N—B3	P—B3

DIAGRAM 148

(after 24 . . . P—B3)
Sequel to a perfect defense:
ho-hum!

* For fork and pin, see *Winning Chess*, p. 43.

The rest of the play is of no interest. It is given only because its very lack of interest clearly indicates that Black has a perfectly safe game. In other words, his defense has been thoroughly satisfactory.

25	N—R2	. . . .

Prudently avoiding 25 P—QN4, N—K5; 26 R—Q7 ch, K—B1 and the threat of . . . N—B6 is troublesome for White.

25	. . . .	K—B1
26	N—N4	K—K2
27	P—B3	R—Q2
28	RxR ch	NxR
29	B—N5	N—B1
30	R—Q2	R—B4
31	B—K2	B—Q4

DIAGRAM 149

(after 31 . . . B—Q4)
Whatever initiative still remains, is in Black's hands.

Black's pieces are posted more aggressively. White's position, though tenable, is uncomfortable.

32	P—R3	B—N6
33	N—B2	N—K3
34	B—Q1	BxB

35	NxB	R—B8
36	K—B2	N—B4
37	N—B3	N—N6
38	R—K2	P—B4

DIAGRAM 150

(after 38 . . . P—B4)
The draw approaches.

The previous comment still applies.

39	N—Q5 *ch*	K—K3
40	P—K4	P—B5
41	N—N4	N—R4
	Drawn	

With this game we conclude our study of Lasker's Defense to the Queen's Gambit Declined.

In the first three games with this defense (Martinez-Guimard, Bonham-Isles and Eliskases-Gruenfeld) we saw Black's Queen Bishop developed along its original diagonal to KN5 after *White* initiated an exchange of Pawns opening up that diagonal.

In the remaining game with this defense (Scheltinga-Grau) we saw Black's Queen Bishop developed on the long diagonal after *Black* exchanged Pawns in the center opening up the long diagonal.

Either method of developing the Bishop was satisfactory. Thus Black solved his great problem in this opening: how to develop the

Queen Bishop satisfactorily. And, as this defense involves preliminary simplification by Black which frees his remaining pieces for action and also affords him *adequate control of the center*, we are justified in concluding that Lasker's Defense can be strongly recommended as a defense that solves the second player's problems in this opening.

♛ PART FOUR ♛

How to Exploit Inferior Play by
Your Opponent

———————————————————————————

CHAPTER 19

What If My Opponent Doesn't Follow the Book?

W E H A V E now concluded our study of three recommended openings. Each of these openings conforms to the requirements for a good opening which we posited in Chapter 1:

(1) *effective and rapid development*
(2) *adequate control of the center*
(3) *permanent validity regardless of fluctuations in theory*

But our task is not completed. We must still consider the question: "What if my opponent doesn't follow the book?" This leads to such questions as: what is inferior play? How do you recognize it as such? What do you do about it?

Broadly speaking, we justifiably assume that whatever is wrong with your opponent's opening play will create a lasting weakness in his armor—a weakness that can be exploited mercilessly in the middle game. *The more flagrant your opponent's mistakes, the easier it is for you to plan the middle game.*

The most important hint you need for future policy is that your opponent's opening mistakes will involve violations of one or more of the principles previously set forth. In other words, your opponent will get a bad development; he will neglect control of the center; he will adopt opening lines which have been known to be bad for decades. The games in the next four chapters will illustrate such mistakes and demonstrate how they are exploited.

Thus, your opponent may neglect to occupy the center with Pawns. In that case, you monopolize the center, getting a splendid development which your opponent cannot emulate. You need not concern yourself with the problem of how the play will proceed twenty or thirty moves later. You can confidently assume that if you monopolize Pawn control of the center, and if you have much the better development, you must inevitably enjoy the opportunity to make use of your advantages. This is not an empty claim: this type of exploitation has been applied in thousands upon thousands of games. It is exemplified in the games given in the following chapters.

Another instance: suppose your opponent makes a move that gives him a cramped game. Then you conclude that your course will be to constrict your opponent's game more and more. Again, you can be confident that the opportunity will be forthcoming to exploit the constricted state of your opponent's game.

Another possibility is that your opponent will develop his pieces to unfavorable squares. In that case, you systematically bring out your pieces quickly and effectively, so that when you are ready to attack at a given point, *you can muster more force for attack than your opponent can assemble for defense.*

Just how, you may ask, is superior force, or superior mobility, employed to force victory? This is the key question which will arise in each of the next four examples, and in each case it will be answered for you in clear-cut, unforgettable fashion.

CHAPTER 20

The Importance of Controlling
the Center

THE FOLLOWING game is very instructive because it shows the clash of ideas between a master and an amateur. The master, playing twenty games in a simultaneous exhibition, has to rely pretty much on general principles, cursory impressions, alert observations and quick conclusions. His opponent is obviously no student of the game, and despite the extra time at his disposal, is truly helpless.

The master has applied general principles so often that they are part of his instantaneous reaction to any given position. His opponent here has no guiding idea and simply flounders. In this game, then, we see:

(1) *how the master applies general principles*
(2) *how his opponent violates general principles*
(3) *how the master punishes his opponent's violations of general principles*

Such games as this one are very instructive. The opening mistakes are so flagrant and their middle game exploitation so striking that you can readily see the links between the opening and the middle game.

QUEEN'S GAMBIT DECLINED
PARIS, 1913

WHITE	BLACK
A. Alekhine	*M. Prat*
1 P—Q4	P—Q4
2 N—KB3	N—QB3

This move is frowned upon by theory because in Queen Pawn openings it is important for either player to be in a position to play his Queen Bishop Pawn two squares. This creates the possibility of *Pawn captures with resulting open files for the Rooks.*

As White plays, he is able to make Pawn captures that open lines for his Rooks.

As Black plays, he is unable to make Pawn captures that open lines for his Rooks.

3   P—B4   . . . .

DIAGRAM 151

(after 3 P—B4)
The struggle for control of
the center begins.

A very important position of a type that is seen repeatedly in modern play. On both sides the Queen Pawn has been advanced to the fourth rank. Both players would like to advance their respective King Pawn likewise to the fourth rank. With both center Pawns in this dominating situation, the opponent's forces could be kept away (or kicked away) from the vital central zone. (How this is accomplished will be seen from the further course of this game.)

So, granting that the advance of the King Pawn is desirable, we note regretfully that this advance is impossible because of the hostile Pawn at Q4. Thus, instead of his last move, White

could not have played 3 P—K4 ? as Black would simply have
played 3 . . . PxP. Hence White had to *prepare* for P—K4.
And there you have the basic idea of the Queen's Gambit:
Black's Queen Pawn at Q4 is an obstacle to the execution of
White's plan calling for a powerful, broad center (White
Pawns on K4 and Q4). White must remove the obstacle (Black
Pawn at Q4). And the way to remove that obstacle is to play
P—QB4. Why?

Well, if Black captures (. . . QPxQBP) the obstacle to
White's P—K4 has been removed. Or, if Black allows the
Queen Pawn to be captured by White, the obstacle likewise
disappears, and White is ready for P—K4.

In practice, Black maintains the obstacle to White's advance
P—K4 *by supporting his Queen Pawn with a Pawn.* In that
event, BPxQP can always be answered by . . . PxP (on the
assumption that White's P—B4 has been answered by . . .
P—K3 or . . . P—QB3).

(*We return now to the position of Diagram 151.*)

3 . . . .   P—K3 ?

Black is playing according to theory, but having violated
theory on the second move, he cannot expect theory to stand
still and benefit him on the third move!

2 . . . N—QB3 is wrong from the point of view of blocking
Black's Queen Bishop Pawn and thus preventing Pawn exchanges by Black, but the move does have another purpose—
a constructive purpose—and this purpose is ignored by Black.

The right sequel to 2 . . . N—QB3 is 3 . . . B—N5, intending . . . BxN and then . . . P—K4. The logic of this is
immediately apparent: White's Queen Pawn on Q4 and Knight
on KB3 are obstacles to Black's desired . . . P—K4. By playing . . . B—N5 Black threatens to remove the main obstacle
to his advancing . . . P—K4.

There is another reason why Black should strive for . . .
P—K4 instead of resigning himself to . . . P—K3. The latter

move blocks the action of his Queen Bishop. In fact, one of the chief problems of modern opening play is the question of developing this Bishop effectively after it is hemmed in during the opening by . . . P—K3. It is this crucial problem which is solved so neatly by Lasker's Defense (Part III).

To sum up the significance of 2 . . . N—QB3:

The move has the drawback of blocking Black's . . . P—QB4. It has the potential advantage of making . . . P—K4 (freedom!) possible. By playing . . . P—K3, as he has just done, Black accentuates the difficulties resulting from the blocking of his Queen Bishop Pawn, and deprives himself of getting some benefit from . . . N—QB3 by freeing himself with . . . P—K4.

DIAGRAM 152

(after 3 . . . P—K3 ?)
Black has made a serious mistake.

During his first three moves, Black has already condemned both Rooks and his Queen Bishop to lasting inactivity. But he does not know that! This is the typical experience of the player who lacks theoretical knowledge: His difficulties in the middle game baffle him and leave him disheartened, all the more so since he does not realize that these difficulties are the result of his violation of general principles in the opening.

4   N—B3   PxP ?

Black seems bent on committing almost every opening mistake conceivable. Having blocked his Queen Bishop with 3 . . . P—K3 in order to set up a permanent obstacle to White's P—K4, he suddenly negates the beneficial effect of 3 . . . P—K3 by capturing White's Queen Bishop Pawn and thus allowing White to obtain a powerful, broad center.

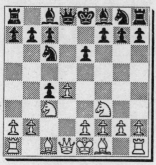

DIAGRAM 153

(after 4 . . . PxP ?)
Black has surrendered control
of the center.

Black's opening play has a sadly ironic quality: having played 2 . . . N—QB3, he is saddled with its drawbacks and derives none of its benefits; having played 3 . . . P—K3, he is again saddled with its drawbacks and derives none of its benefits!

5 P—K3   . . . .

Here the master makes an inexact move, not to be wondered at since he is playing so many games. The right way is 5 P—K4 (winning the Queen Bishop Pawn just as he does after the text) and also preventing Black from getting a foothold in the center.

This last point is very important: after 5 P—K4 White has a powerful, broad center, so that if 5 . . . N—B3; 6 BxP Black cannot play 6 . . . B—Q3 (with a view to . . . P—K4), for

then the crushing 7 P—K5 wins a piece! Compare this with the
note to White's sixth move.

| | 5 | . . . . | N—B3 |
| | 6 | BxP | . . . . |

DIAGRAM 154

(after 6 BxP)
Black can still fight for a fair
share of the center.

And now Black, despite his previous blunders, can still make
a fight of it with 6 . . . B—Q3 ! intending 7 . . . P—K4 ! If
Black can advance the King Pawn his pieces will have a firm
foothold in the center, his Queen Bishop can be developed
effectually, his King Rook will have a useful half-open file on
the King file.

In reply to 6 . . . B—Q3 ! White is virtually forced to play
7 B—N5 (despite the loss of a move involved) in order to pin
Black's Queen Knight * and thus prevent . . . P—K4. But
then Black unpins with 7 . . . Castles and again threatens to
play . . . P—K4 even at the cost of sacrificing a Pawn in some
variations.

It comes down to this: if Black can get a Pawn in the center
(at Q4 and/or K4) his game has backbone, his pieces have
security and mobility. *If the center is not occupied or com-*

* For the pin, see *Winning Chess*, p. 7.

manded by him, he is doomed to be the victim of a fatal squeeze—which is just what happens in this game.

(*We return now to the position of Diagram 154.*)

6 . . . .   B—N5
7 Castles   BxN

As Black's game is already very bad, there is no point in criticizing his moves on the ground that he might have had better ones—he no longer has good moves at his disposal! That is really the meaning of a bad position: *it does not offer scope for good moves, good plans, good ideas, good attack, good defense.* Only good opening play leaves us the possibility of playing well later on.

About Black's last move, then, we merely note that it leaves White with two Bishops against Bishop and Knight. The effect of this will be appraised following the next diagram.

8 PxB   . . . .

DIAGRAM 155

(after 8 PxB)
White's Bishops will have tremendous scope.

The exchange of pieces has strengthened White's center: his Queen Bishop Pawn supports the Queen Pawn.

More important, however, is the fact that White has acquired a new diagonal for his Queen Bishop. This piece can play to QR3, sweeping down the diagonal QR3—KB8 with terrific power. Thus White's possession of two Bishops against Bishop and Knight gives him a really significant advantage. With both Bishops trained powerfully against Black's center and King-side, White will soon be seeking new avenues of attack.

>8   . . . .   **Castles**
>9   Q—B2   . . . .

Preparing to advance the King Pawn: P—K4, then P—K5 driving off Black's King Knight from its most useful square.

>9   . . . .   N—K2

And this other Knight has no good square, no good prospects.

>*10*   B—R3   . . . .

In contrast to Black's miserable Knights, White's Bishops have magnificent scope.

DIAGRAM 156

(after 10 B—R3)
White is ready to plan for the
middle game.

White is already in a position to formulate his general plan of the game.

By advancing P—K4 and (after removing his Knight) P—KB4 White will establish a formidable Pawn center which will stifle all counterplay on Black's part.

White will then post all his pieces on favorable squares—a procedure that Black cannot possibly imitate!—and will then be ready for the final onslaught. How that concluding phase will come about is for the moment unclear to us; yet the plan has been formed, and will be executed, in the staunch faith that *the twofold advantage of overwhelming center and overwhelmingly superior development must lead to a crushing victory for White.*

10 . . . .   P—B3

The natural move in such situations is . . . P—B4, which would have the merits of putting some counterpressure on White's center; breaking the diagonal of White's Queen Bishop; giving Black's Queen Rook a half-open file at QB1 and in general giving Black's pieces more maneuvering space.

But this natural and highly desirable advance of the Queen Bishop Pawn to QB4 is quite out of the question, in consequence of a number of faulty Black moves, of which the first was 2 . . . N—QB3.

If White's coming success is to be credited to good and consistent planning, then Black's coming failure can be charged to faulty planning, or none at all.

11 P—K4   P—KR3

Pawn advances in front of the castled King make it easy for the opponent to attack with assurance of success. However, Black has little choice, for such a weakness can always be forced by White; for example, by White's threat of playing 12 P—K5 (driving away Black's Knight from KB3) and then 13 N—N5 or 13 B—Q3.

(In the Morphy-Lewis game—Chapter 22—, by the way, we have a similar example of how the existence of a Pawn weakness in the castled King's position facilitates the enemy's attack.)

Thus we again see the consequences of bad opening play: the early mistakes weaken the power of resistance to where the player under attack *has* to create weaknesses, even if he knows enough to *want* to avoid them.

12   QR—Q1   . . . .

The Rook is brought into contact with the rest of White's forces. At this very moment White does not know just how the Rook is going to be used; but, as a master of long experience, he can see that a violent attack is building up, and that the Rook is bound to play a useful role in this attack.

12   . . . .   B—Q2

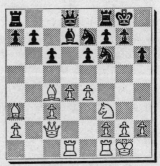

Diagram 157

(after 12 . . . B—Q2)
Black's pieces cannot function
effectively.

Contrast the wretched position of Black's Queen Bishop with the splendid posts available to White's Bishops. This comparison should make clear the effects of Black's bad opening moves on the fate of his Queen Bishop. As a result of Black's mistakes in the opening, his Bishop is condemned to uselessness throughout the game.

13   N—K5   . . . .

Now the Knight acquires a beautifully aggressive outpost position! Note how White has good squares for his pieces, and gets even better squares for them, without trying. The good moves seem to come of themselves. Why? The answer is that *just as bad opening play makes subsequent good moves almost impossible, so good opening play creates a very favorable basis for good moves later on.*

13   . . . .   R—K1

Black wants to move his Queen, which was previously impossible because the Knight at K2 had to be protected. Hence the Rook move, which frees the Queen for "action" that is very sadly limited.

DIAGRAM 158

(after 13 . . . R—K1)
How can White open new
lines?

White has achieved an impeccable development, and his position has more or less reached the height of its power.

Here is the moment of decision: having this powerful position, how does White proceed? How does he attack? How does he turn all his superior development to account? What use does he make of his control of the center?

What is needed is more line-opening. This is the characteristic solution in most positions of this kind. Black is skulking on three ranks, his pieces huddled together miserably, accomplishing little. Yet there he is. The only way to smoke him out, to document his helplessness, to exploit the enormous charge of explosive potential that White has built up, is *to open up new lines*. Hence we look for Pawn captures. None are available. What now?

The answer to all of White's questions is *the advance of his King Bishop Pawn*. By playing P—B4 and then P—B5 White will prepare for a decisive augmentation of his attack: pressure on the King Bishop file, pressure on the diagonal from QR2—

Figure 14

White has overwhelming control of the center, and his pieces are magnificently posted. The way to make conclusive use of these advantages is to open an attacking line. Hence the advance of White's King Bishop Pawn is indicated.

KN8—the diagonal on which his King Bishop is placed. Note that the attacking potential of White's Rook on KB1, of his Bishop on QB4 and of his Knight on K5 will all converge on a common target: the square KB7, on which Black's King Bishop Pawn is placed.

14   P—B4 !   Q—B2

Black is merely marking time. There is nothing he can do of any significance to counteract the execution of White's plan.

15   P—B5 !   QR—Q1

DIAGRAM 159

(after 15 . . . QR—Q1)
White is ready to break
through.

White has many ways to win in this position. Alekhine chooses the most spectacular, a method so brilliant that an ordinary player would never dream of it. But precisely because this finish is so flamboyant, it underlines the vast superiority of White's game.

16   NxKBP !   . . . .

This sacrifice disposes drastically of the problem of how to exploit Black's Achilles heel (his KB2).

16   . . . .   KxN
17   P—K5   . . . .

DIAGRAM 160

(after 17 P—K5)
Black has no good defense.

With this crushing central advance, White exacts the final
penalty for Black's surrender of the center (4 . . . PxP ?).

Should Black move his attacked Knight, the following would
be a plausible conclusion: 17 . . . N/B3—Q4; 18 PxP *dbl ch*,
KxP; 19 BxN/K2, KxB (if 19 . . . RxB; 20 Q—B5 mate); 20
Q—N6 and Black is quite helpless against the threats of 21
Q—B7 mate; or 21 R—B7 mate; or 21 QxP *ch* followed by 22
Q—B7 mate or 22 Q—B6 mate or 22 R—B6 mate! (Note that
in these variations, Black's Knight at Q4 is pinned most of the
time and therefore useless.*)

(*We return now to the position of Diagram 160.*)

17 . . . .   N/K2—N1

Black repentantly offers back the extra piece, but White is
out for blood.

18 B—Q6   Q—B1
19 Q—K2 !   . . . .

Of course Black must not move the menaced Knight, for
then 20 Q—R5 *ch* forces mate. (*See Diagram 161.*)

19 . . . .   P—QN4
20 B—N3   P—QR4

* For the pin, see *Winning Chess*, p. 7.

DIAGRAM 161

(after 19 Q—K2 !)
Black is helpless!

Black tries feverishly to drive away the Bishop, but it is too late.

21   QR—K1 ! !   . . . .

Planning an announced ten-move mate!

21   . . . .   P—R5

DIAGRAM 162

(after 21 . . . P—R5)
Now Black succumbs to a
masterly Queen sacrifice.

White now announced mate in ten moves. Here is the procedure:

| 22 | Q—R5 *ch !!* | NxQ |
| 23 | PxP *dbl ch* ° | K—N3 |

Forced.

| 24 | B—B2 *ch* | K—N4 |
| 25 | R—B5 *ch* | K—N3 |

If 25 . . . K—N5; 26 P—R3 *ch* leads to a quick mate; like-wise if 25 . . . . K—R5; 26 R—K4 *ch.*

26	R—B6 *dbl ch*	K—N4
27	R—N6 *ch*	K—R5
28	R—K4 *ch*	N—B5
29	RxN *ch*	K—R4
30	P—N3 *!*	. . . .

DIAGRAM 163

(after 30 P—N3 *!*)
With a whole Queen ahead,
Black cannot prevent mate
next move!

And now, *no matter what Black plays,* there follows 31 R—R4 mate! Black's helplessness, even with a whole Queen ahead, gives us some idea of the fury of the storm unleashed by Black's faulty opening play (neglected control of the center).

° For double check, see *Winning Chess,* p. 85.

This game is a graphic sermon on the importance of controlling the center. It must be controlled by Pawns in most cases, occasionally by pieces. For the average player, Pawn control is the more reliable method by far.

Black's neglect of the center made it impossible for his pieces to occupy effective posts in or near the center. His forces had little scope. They were steadily driven back by White's step-by-step encroachments. When the decisive turn arrived at move 14, White resorted to a dynamic Pawn advance which ensured a quick opening up of vital lines of attack. Two moves later the stage was set for a crushing sacrificial attack.

It is no exaggeration to say that at move 21 White's center Pawns are worth more than the Black Queen! The moral, then, for the chapters that follow, is:

Play for control of the center! With center control you are assured of quick, easy, effective development. Neglecting center control, you will find that your development is slow, tortuous, ineffectual.

CHAPTER 21

How Superior Mobility Leads
to a Stormy Breakthrough

Aᴌᴌ ᴄʜᴇssᴘʟᴀʏᴇʀs love to see beautiful games which abound in dazzling sacrifices. The following game is particularly enjoyable, as it is one of the most brilliant games ever played. Such games delight us with their refreshing, colorful qualities, so far removed from the ordinary run of games.

But our aim is learning and not mere enjoyment. We must realize, therefore, that all chess brilliancy embodies a profound lesson: *sound combinations always spring from defects in the opponent's play.* Beautiful as White's sacrifices are, they originate in the accumulated effects of Black's previous mistakes: his cramped position; his faulty development; his weakened black squares; his inability to shield his King adequately; the impossibility of his rallying and regrouping his forces as White piles sacrifice upon sacrifice.

Remove these flaws in Black's play, and you make White's sacrifices impossible! That is the vital lesson to be learned from this lovely game. *In chess, the highest flights of artistry are conditioned by the opponent's previous blunders!*

KING FIANCHETTO DEFENSE
MERAN, 1926

WHITE	BLACK
D. Przepiorka	J. von Patay
1 P—Q4	P—KN3

As in the next two games, Black opens irregularly; he intends to "fianchetto" his King Bishop—play it to KN2. This is

satisfactory procedure only if he combines it with Pawn occupation of the center. Failure to occupy the center will leave
this vital area at the mercy of White's forces.

2   P—K4   . . . .

By setting up his center Pawns on the fourth rank, White
opens lines for the quick, easy development of his pieces and
at the same time automatically prevents Black from posting
pieces on the important center squares.

2 . . . .   P—Q3

Black, on the other hand, is holding back. Even at this early
stage we can forecast that White's pieces will be free and
active; Black's, cramped and passive.

DIAGRAM 164

(after 2 . . . P—Q3)

Black has voluntarily condemned himself to a cramped
game!

3   N—KB3   . . . .

White develops the Knight to its best square and at the
same time prepares for castling.

3 . . . .   B—N2
4   B—Q3   . . . .

Many players would prefer B—QB4 here, in order to post this Bishop on the fine diagonal leading to Black's KB2.

The text development is perhaps a shade inferior, although, as it happens, the development of the Bishop to Q3 turns out to be wonderfully effective in this game.

In any event, the development of the Bishop is the necessary prelude to early castling, assuring the safety of White's King.

DIAGRAM 165

(after 4 B—Q3)
Black must fight for control
of the center.

4 . . . .   P—K3 ?

Here Black is at fault. Unless he establishes a foothold in the center, he will be inexorably ground down by White's superior development.

The proper course was therefore 4 . . . P—K4. If then 5 PxP, PxP or 5 P—B3, N—QB3 or 5 P—Q5, N—KB3 and Black is by no means badly off. (As soon as Black gets a solid position in the center, his prospects for satisfactory development brighten perceptibly!)

5 Castles   N—K2

If Black plays the Knight to its natural square KB3, he will always have to fear P—K5, driving the Knight into oblivion.

Had he played the proper fourth move (4 . . . P—K4) he would not have to worry about finding the best placement for his King Knight.

Thus the consequence of his taking a passive position in the center (. . . P—K3 instead of . . . P—K4) is that he must resign himself to an inferior position for his King Knight (. . . N—K2 instead of . . . N—KB3).

> 6 B—K3   . . . .

A sound developing move. White contemplates Q—Q2 followed by B—KR6 with a view to removing Black's King Bishop. If the protective Bishop disappears, the weak black squares on the King-side will form welcome targets for White's attack.

> 6 . . . .   Castles
> 7 Q—Q2   . . . .

DIAGRAM 166

(after 7 Q—Q2)
Black does not relish the possibility of B—KR6.

White is intent on playing B—KR6, forcing the exchange of Bishops, so that he can get to work on Black's weakened black squares.

> 7 . . . .   R—K1
> 8 B—KR6   B—R1

Black has avoided the exchange of Bishops, but his position presents a miserable appearance. Not one of his pieces functions effectively, and he is apparently doomed to maneuver rather helplessly on the back ranks.

DIAGRAM 167

(after 8 . . . B—R1)
Black's development is slow
and cramped.

9   N—B3   . . . .

White, on the other hand, continues to develop effortlessly.

9   . . . .   QN—B3

Black's first aggressive developing move! White's Queen Pawn is doubly attacked.

10   N—K2   P—Q4 ?

The wrong center Pawn. Even now he should still try . . . P—K4, opening up the diagonal of his Queen Bishop.

11   P—K5 !   . . . .

After the advance of White's King Pawn, we can consider that the course of the coming middle game has been determined once for all. Hence it is possible, after inspection of this position, to forecast the correct strategy for White. What are the factors that will enter into this appraisal?

DIAGRAM 168

(after 11 P—K5 !)
Note the vulnerable black
squares on Black's King-side.

(1) Black's development is wretched, and there is no way
in which this defect can be remedied. The Knights have no
prospects; the Queen Bishop has no proper diagonal; the King
Bishop guards the miserably weak black squares on the King-
side, but aside from that has little more than the mobility of a
Pawn; Black's Rooks have no files on which to operate; his
Queen can barely move off the first rank and certainly has no
opportunity for aggressive deployment.

(2) As has been indicated, the black squares on Black's
King-side are seriously weak and offer fine nesting-places for
the White forces. Thus White can effectively occupy KN5 or
KB6 without any danger of being driven away by a hostile
Pawn.

(3) White, it goes without saying, has no weaknesses whatever in his Pawn structure.

(4) White has a magnificent development. His Pawns at K5
and Q4 choke off any possibility of rational development for
Black, and at the same time they form a barrier behind which
White can maneuver his pieces for attacking purposes.

(5) White's Queen, Knights and Bishops are all aggressively
posted, and there are several ways to bring his Rooks into the

game. One way would be by means of QR—K1 and then R—
K3 and eventually R—R3. Another way would be P—KB4
(after due preparation) followed by P—KN4 with a view to an
ultimate P—B5. As in the previous game, the line-opening by
means of Pawn exchanges (in this case, the opening of the
King Bishop file after P—KB5) should prove decisive.

(6) Another attacking method at White's disposal is P—B3
(to prevent a subsequent . . . N—N5) followed by P—KN4
(to prevent a subsequent . . . N—B4) and Q—B4 with N—
N5 as the clincher.

With these attacking ideas in the air, White has his future
course tidily mapped out for him. All this is clear enough to
Black, who consequently tries to fight back while he still has
some fight left in his wretched position.

(*We return now to the position of Diagram 168.*)

| 11 | . . . . | N—B4 |
| 12 | B—KB4 | . . . . |

He does not permit the exchange . . . NxB etc. as Black's
Knight will soon be driven away from B4. Besides, the Bishop
will be useful from the point of view of attacking the weak
black squares in Black's camp.

DIAGRAM 169

(after 12 B—KB4)
White avoids simplification.

| 12 | . . . . | P—B3 |

As the present is dark and the future darker, he decides to anticipate White's coming offensive by a desperate attempt at counterplay.

Even though this attempt is doomed to fail, Black is right in taking this stand. He must try to break White's grip on the center before his Knight is driven from B4 and he is subsequently strangled. If Black's attempt fails, that merely means that everything he tries, must necessarily fail. *A bad opening results in a bad middle game.*

DIAGRAM 170

(after 12 . . . P—B3)
Black sets a trap.

Black has an interesting positional trap in view. He hopes for 13 P—KN4, which he will meet in this surprising fashion: 13 . . . N/B4xP *!;* 14 N/K2xN, NxN; 15 NxN, PxP forking two pieces and regaining his temporarily sacrificed piece with a much improved position.*

Thus we see how one incautious move on White's part dissipates much of his advantage. And what, incidentally, is the nature of this "incautious move"? It is simply this: *White's advantage is based on his monopoly of the center. If this monopoly is smashed, much of his advantage disappears as well.*

(*We return now to the position of Diagram 170.*)

* For double attacks with the Pawn push, see *Winning Chess*, p. 61.

13   P—B3 !   . . . .

White takes good care to maintain the center in all its
formidable solidity.

DIAGRAM 171

(after 13 P—B3 !)
White has seen through
Black's plan.

The effect of White's last move is that the sturdiness of his
center setup is maintained; no *Putsch* is possible in the center;
his Knight at K2 is relieved of its defensive duties; and Black
is still badly tied up.

13   . . . .   P—KN4 ? ?

Black's naivete is appalling. He expects the attacked Bishop
to retreat, after which he will play . . . P—N5, driving off
White's King Knight and winning the King Pawn.

This is the crisis for White. Is he to allow Black to win the
Pawn and—what is more important—allow the breakup of
White's proud center?

Or is White to stick to his plan, which was to play for King-
side attack, to press on the weak black squares, to keep Black
constricted as in a vise?

Naturally White wants to play according to plan; but this
requires a sacrifice. So here we come to a most instructive

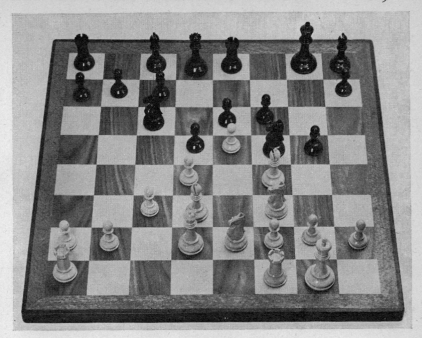

Figure 15

The game has reached the crucial stage. White seems compelled to retreat his attacked Bishop; but retreat will result in the dissolution of his powerful center. Hence White's coming combination is really the continuation of his previous strategical planning.

point: to the novice, the sacrifice which follows seems to be sheer inspiration. *Actually the sacrifice is more prosaic than that: it is evoked by White's previously formulated plan of the game!*

Of course, we are not interested here in the clash between the inspired and the prosaic. What is more important to us is the realization that *a bad plan leads to drift and self-doubt; a good plan brings good moves in its train.*

14	NxP !	PxN
15	BxP	. . . .

DIAGRAM 172

(after 13 . . . P—KN4 ? ?)
White must make a crucial
decision.

DIAGRAM 173

(after 15 BxP)
What has White accom-
plished with his sacrifice?

White has only two Pawns for the piece—generally inadequate compensation.

But other factors have to be taken into account: Black's
King is no longer shielded by a rampart of protective Pawns;
Black's pieces are still ineffectual, and this factor alone is
enough to nullify Black's academic material superiority; White
can get a "Pawn-roller" moving—P—KN4 followed by P—KB4
and P—B5—with the result that Black's pieces will be kicked

around and a rational development will become impossible for
him.

15 ....   Q—Q2

This protects the second rank—at least for the time being—
but has the drawback of postponing to an even later stage the
development of Black's Queen Bishop. However, Black has no
move which is wholly satisfactory.

If 15 . . . N/B4—K2; 16 Q—B2 enables White to pick off a
third Pawn, completing the denuding of Black's King.

Or if 15 . . . N/B3—K2; 16 P—KN4, N—N2; 17 Q—B2
with the same result as in the previous variation.

Note that the natural move 15 . . . B—B3 is impossible because of White's unshakable grip on the important square KB6.

16 P—KN4 !   ....

Very disagreeable for Black.

DIAGRAM 174

(after 16 P—KN4 !)
How is Black to answer the
attack on his Knight?

If now 16 . . . N—N2 or 16 . . . N/B4—K2; 17 Q—B2
wins another Pawn while the attack rages undiminished.

Still another way—and perhaps even more effective—is 17
P—KB4 followed by 18 P—B5 with a crushing "Pawn-roller"
attack.

Not caring for either of these possibilities, Black tries another way.

(*We return now to the position of Diagram 174.*)

16	. . . .	P—KR3
17	PxN *!*	. . . .

White is not interested in a Pawn more or less. After 17 BxP, NxB; 18 QxN, Q—N2; 19 Q—R5, B—Q2; 20 P—KB4 (still the "Pawn-roller"!) White is bound to win; but he wants to find an even faster way to victory.

17	. . . .	PxB

With a faint hope of 18 QxP *ch*, Q—N2 and Black forces the exchange of Queens putting an end to White's attack.

18	P—B6 *!*	. . . .

DIAGRAM 175

(after 18 P—B6 *!*)
Black's pieces are clumsily
situated for defensive purposes.

The forward thrust of the King Bishop Pawn is the logical continuation of the attack.

Black's pieces are still cramped for maneuvering space and find it more difficult than ever to come to the aid of the endangered Black King. The immediate threat is 19 QxP *ch* followed by 20 N—B4.

(*We return now to the position of Diagram 175.*)

18 . . . .   K—B2

Setting a little trap: if 19 QxP *P P*, R—KN1 pins * and wins White's Queen. In any case, Black hopes to gain time for . . . R—KN1 with a semblance of defense.

DIAGRAM 176

(after 18 . . . K—B2)
White continues with an astounding sacrifice.

Black's position suddenly seems quite solid. Shall we therefore conclude that White's basic plan was wrong, or that his execution of the plan was faulty?

Before we observe very shortly that Black's "security" is nothing but a pitiful sham, let us quickly review what White has been trying to accomplish. He is combining a severe constriction policy with a raking King-side attack, relying for success on the exposed position of Black's King and the congested development of Black's pieces.

At move 17 he had a fairly clear and easy win, which he turned down in favor of a much quicker, more sensational method. Both procedures are correct and decisive; so we con-

* For the pin see *Winning Chess*, p. 7.

clude that White's plan was right, his execution of the plan appropriate and pointed.

19   B—N6 ch ! ! ! . . . .

The first of a series of stunning surprises. Instead of relying on a "Pawn-roller" attack, he intends to force open the King Knight file all the way, with grievous consequences for Black's King.

DIAGRAM 177

(after 19 B—N6 ch ! ! !)
A nasty shock for Black!

White's first object in sacrificing the Bishop so spectacularly is to gain time: a check must always be respected, and thus Black is left no time for playing . . . R—KN1.

19 . . . .   KxB

After 19 . . . K—B1; 20 QxP White has an easy win by simply piling up more force for attack than Black can assemble for defense.

20   Q—Q3 ch ! . . . .

The peremptory checks continue, and at the same time White prepares the switch of his all-powerful Queen to the King-side.

20 . . . .   K—R3

20 . . . K—R4 leads to the same position.

If instead 20 . . . K—B2; 21 Q—R7 *ch,* K—B1; 22 QxB *ch,*
K—B2; 23 Q—N7 mate.

21   **Q—R3** *ch*   **K—N3**

And now 22 N—N3 looks strong, but 22 . . . Q—R2 *!* is a
more than satisfactory reply. Something more inspired is called
for!

DIAGRAM 178

(after 21 . . . K—N3)
Another brilliant sacrifice is
in order!

22   **N—B4** *ch ! ! !* . . . .

A strikingly brilliant way of opening the King Knight file.
Black must take, for 22 . . . K—B2 allows a quick mate (23
Q—R7 *ch* etc.).

22   . . . .   **PxN**
23   **K—R1** *! !*   . . . .

This "quiet" move prepares for a devastating Rook check on
the newly-opened file. (*See Diagram 179.*)

Black is helpless. Thus if 23 . . . Q—R2; 24 R—N1 *ch* and
mate in two more moves.

23   . . . .   **BxP**

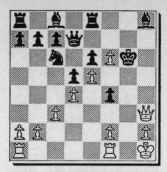

DIAGRAM 179

(after 23 K—R1 *! !*)
The quiet King move presages
disaster for Black.

Desperately hoping to be able to escape after 24 PxB, KxP
etc. But White has better.

24   R—N1 *ch !*   B—N4

Or 24 . . . K—B2; 25 Q—R7 *ch* and mate next move.

DIAGRAM 180

(after 24 . . . B—N4)
Now comes the final sacrifice!

25   RxB *! !*   . . . .

The fourth sacrifice!

25   . . . .   KxR
26   R—N1 mate

Black is three pieces ahead, but they are of little importance, posted inactively as they are.

White's basic plan (constriction plus violent breakthrough) has carried the day. As in the previous game, we see that adequate control of the center is the first requirement for satisfactory development and reasonably certain protection against quick defeat.

In both games, Black's failure to get an adequate share of the center resulted in the posting of his pieces on squares where they functioned very poorly. This in turn led to a constricted situation in which the pieces got in each other's way.

With Black's forces in both instances operating far below their optimum strength, Black was helpless against the flood of sacrifices which set in as soon as White had completed his development. The faulty placement of the Black pieces cut off effective communication with the King-side, and a virtually naked Black King was exposed to the raging fury of an attack conducted with the full cooperation of White's splendidly posted pieces.

Such is the indicated conclusion of a middle game which results from a very poorly played opening.

CHAPTER 22

How Line-opening Leads to Attacking Possibilities

W<small>E HAVE</small> already had occasion to note in quite a few games that Pawn captures result in open lines. In the following game such line-opening (along the King Bishop file) is particularly impressive.

What Morphy accomplishes with the open file is a miracle of attacking technique. The file is used as a supply highway to convey White pieces to the King-side. As the White pieces utilize this highway, the attack is automatically intensified.

As in Chapters 20 and 21, we note that Black's shabby development and early surrender of the center leave him with no opportunity to deploy *his* pieces in the same forceful manner.

A word about the opening: you are asked to think of it as beginning in the following manner: 1 P—Q4, P—QN3; 2 P—K4. That is, White begins with 1 P—Q4 and when his opponent fails to dispute the center, White continues 2 P—K4. (Of course, the great Morphy had no use for 1 P—Q4, and this attitude is so well publicized that we would not dare to reverse the order of the opening moves!)

QUEEN FIANCHETTO DEFENSE
PHILADELPHIA, 1859

WHITE	BLACK
P. Morphy	*S. Lewis*
1 P—K4	P—QN3

Black repeats the mistake we saw in the earlier games: he allows White to monopolize the center with his Pawns, so that

Black's pieces will be unable to find a foothold in the center later on.

2	P—Q4	B—N2
3	B—Q3	. . . .

White saves time: he defends the menaced King Pawn with a developing move.

Although we generally recommend developing Knights before Bishops, the text is satisfactory because we know that Q3 is the Bishop's best square in this opening. Once Black has castled King-side, the Bishop on Q3 can join in a powerful attacking formation. (See the Diagram after 5 P—K5.)

3	. . . .	P—K3
4	N—KR3 !	. . . .

Black's neglect of the center (1 . . . P—QN3) does him a lot of harm. White's neglect of the center (4 N—KR3) does him no harm at all! Why?

By playing N—KR3, White leaves a path open for the advance of his King Bishop Pawn. (Note how the subsequent P—KB4 and P—B5 opens up the King Bishop file for White's attacking forces later on.)

4	. . . .	P—Q4
5	P—K5	. . . .

Black has made a belated bid for a share of the center, and the results will be unsatisfactory for him.

Black's opening play is so radically wrong that even at this early stage, White can already devise his basic plan for the ensuing middle game. Here are the factors on which that plan is based:

Black's Bishop at N2 is blocked by his own Pawn at Q4. With all its effectiveness choked off by the obstructing Queen Pawn, the Bishop has very little value.

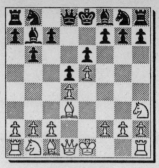

DIAGRAM 181

(after 5 P—K5)
White's last move determines
the course of the middle
game!

On the other hand, White's Bishop at Q3 has a magnificent diagonal headed toward the castled position which will eventually be occupied by Black's King.

One of the best defenses for a castled King is to post a Knight at KB3. In this position, . . . N—KB3 has been prevented by White's P—K5. This enables us to foresee that White will have good attacking chances.

How about White's Knight at KR3? Generally a Knight is badly placed at the side of the board, but here the Knight has good squares at his disposal (N—B4 or N—N5).

Above all, *White can open a powerful attacking line with P—KB4 and P—B5.* This advance is the key to the coming attack.

5 . . . .   N—K2

The Knight is pretty ineffectual here. But, having neglected to establish a foothold in the center, Black is already beginning to pay the penalty in the form of constricted and inadequate development.

6 Castles   N—N3

Black has taken two moves to develop this Knight, and it cannot be said that he has achieved a great deal thereby. However, the Knight moves in order to make way for the development of the King Bishop, which, by the way, will not be very impressive when it comes to pass. Black's neglect of the center is brought home to him move after move.

7 P—KB4 !   . . . .

White intends to use the King Bishop file for attacking purposes. This is accomplished by advancing the Pawn twice to KB5, leading to the opening of the file.

7 . . . .   B—K2
8 P—B5 !   . . . .

DIAGRAM 182

(after 8 P—B5 !)
White forces the opening of
the King Bishop file.

In the above diagram, you observe that an exchange of Pawns is about to take place. *Pawn captures are the most important and most frequent cause of line-opening in chess.*

The play that follows, will show you how to build up the attack on an open file. Looking back for a moment to the early opening play, we see how accurately Morphy appraised the chances of opening the King Bishop file after 4 N—KR3.

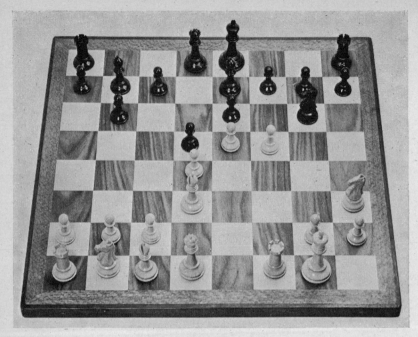

Figure 16

One of the many instances in this book in which we see the effects of line-opening through Pawn capture. The advance 8 P—B5 ! opens the King Bishop file for White, and this gives him the basis for a lasting and decisive attack.

8	. . . .	PxP
9	BxP	B—QB1
10	BxB	QxB
11	N—B3	. . . .

He develops with gain of time by attacking the Queen Pawn. Note how White develops with free-and-easy moves which come of themselves and are most effective. Black, on the other hand, has to resort to tortuous maneuvers which accomplish little. This significant difference arises from the fact that *White monopolizes the center, while Black has no strong point there.*

DIAGRAM 183

(after 11 N—B3)
Black must neglect his development to stop to protect the Queen Pawn.

In the higher sense, Black is already lost: he will never make good his losses in development.

11	. . . .	P—QB3
12	B—N5	Castles
13	BxB	NxB
14	Q—R5 !	. . . .

DIAGRAM 184

(after 14 Q—R5 !)
White's attack is going full blast!

White plays the Queen to its most aggressive post, with a direct menace to Black's castled position. (Note that Black's Queen has no analogous attacking possibility, and is in fact far from the scene of action.)

The more you study this situation, the more threatening White's formation appears. He has 15 N—KN5 in view, menacing mate on the move. After 15 . . . P—KR3 (to stop the mate), 16 NxBP wins a Pawn for White.

This last possibility highlights another important attacking method at White's disposal: the open King Bishop file. And this file is open because White did not block his King Bishop Pawn (4 N—KR3 instead of 4 N—KB3) and because he deliberately played for the opening of the file (7 P—KB4 followed by 8 P—B5).

(*We return now to the position of Diagram 184.*)

14 . . . .   **P—KR3**

Black plays to prevent 15 N—KN5. (*See Diagram 185.*)

He does not have much choice; if, for example, 14 . . . P—N3 15 Q—R6, N—B4; 16 RxN *!*, QxR; 17 N—KN5, R—K1; 18 QxRP *ch*, K—B1; 19 R—KB1 *!* making triumphant use of the open King Bishop file. If now 19 . . . QxN; 20 QxP mate or 20 RxP mate, or if 19 . . . QxR *ch*; 20 KxQ with an easy win.

If 14 . . . Q—K3 White strengthens his attack decisively by doubling Rooks on the open King file. Here is a sample: 14 . . . Q—K3; 15 R—B3 *!*, N—Q2; 16 QR—KB1, P—B3; 17 N—B4 *!*, Q—B4; 18 QxQ, NxQ; 19 N—K6 attacking Rook and Knight and winning the exchange. Or 17 . . . Q—B2; 18 QxQ *ch* followed by P—K6 winning a piece.

15 R—B3 *!*   . . . .

He prepares to strengthen the pressure on the open King Bishop file by doubling Rooks on that line.

Also, he has in mind the possibility of playing R—N3 with the threat of QxRP. (This is an interesting example of how

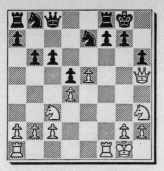

DIAGRAM 185

(after 14 . . . P—KR3)
It is time for White to begin
utilizing the King Bishop file.

Pawn advances in front of the castled King can weaken the
whole castled position.)

        15 . . . .   N—N3

DIAGRAM 186

(after 15 . . . N—N3)
Black hopes to block a frontal
attack on his King.

Black's last move takes some pressure off his King Bishop
Pawn by blocking the attack of the White Queen on that
Pawn; it also removes the threat of QxRP after White's R—N3,
as Black's King Knight Pawn would no longer be pinned.

        16 QR—KB1 !   Q—K3

DIAGRAM 187

(after 16 . . . Q—K3)
Black masses his defensive
forces as best he can.

Both sides have assembled in force on the King-side. White
has a distinct advantage because both of his Rooks are in the
attack, whereas Black has the services of only one Rook for
defensive purposes. However, Black is safe for the moment. In
other words, White's attack needs new power. How is it to get
that new power?

Most players with the White pieces would now play N—B4.
But Morphy's method is much finer: to carry out this exchange,
he transfers his *currently inactive* Knight from QB3 to the
King-side! Remarkably logical play!

> 17   N—K2 !   N—Q2

Black develops a new piece, but it is cursed with the same
fatal drawback that afflicts all of Black's developing moves: *his
failure to control any part of the center* dooms the newly developed Knight to uselessness.

> 18   N/K2—B4 !   NxN
> 19   NxN   Q—K2

Now we see the effect of Morphy's cleverly executed exchange maneuver. White's preponderance of force on the
King-side has been increased, Black's protective Knight has

DIAGRAM 188

(after 19 . . . Q—K2)
White's attack is gaining mo-
mentum.

disappeared and his King's position is stripped bare against the
following powerful attack.

20   R—KN3   . . . .

With Black's protective Knight gone, this threatens QxRP.

20   . . . .   K—R2

Parries the threat.

21   R/B1—B3 !   . . . .

Superior mobility has this insidious quality, that one infiltration leads to another. . . .

White's threat is 22 RxP *ch!*, KxR; 23 R—N3 *ch*, K—R2;
24 R—KR3 and wins, for if 24 . . . Q—N4; 25 QxQ and the
Pawn is pinned.*

Another aspect of the threat is 22 RxP *ch!*, KxR; 23 R—
N3 *ch*, Q—N4; 24 RxQ *ch*, PxR; 25 QxNP *ch*, K moves; 26 Q—
R4 *ch* or Q—R5 *ch*, K moves; 27 Q—N4 *ch* winning the Knight
by double attack.**

(*See Diagram 189.*)

21   . . . .   R—KN1

* For the pin, see *Winning Chess*, p. 7.
** For double attack, see *Winning Chess*, p. 50.

DIAGRAM 189

(after 21 R/B1—B3 !)
White has made good use of
the King Bishop file.

He tries to avoid the weakening of the King's position that
results from 21 . . . P—N3. For in that case White wins by
22 NxNP, PxN; 23 RxP etc.

                22   N—R3 !   . . . .

White's threat is now 23 N—N5 ch, K—R1; 24 NxP ch, K—
R2; 25 Q—N6 mate!

                22   . . . .   P—N3
                23   N—N5 ch !   . . . .

DIAGRAM 190

(after 23 N—N5 ch !)
The final onslaught!

Now the Pawn weaknesses of the castled position take their toll. If 23 . . . K—N2; 24 RxP *ch*, QxR; 25 NxQ winning easily, as White's Queen is immune from capture because of the pin.*

(*We return now to the position of Diagram 190.*)

23   . . . .   QxN
24   RxP *ch*   . . . .

DIAGRAM 191

(after 24 RxP *ch*)
Black's Queen is lost.

24   . . . .   **K—R1**

DIAGRAM 192

(after 24 . . . K—R1)
A neat finesse ends it all.

* For the pin, see *Winning Chess*, p. 7.

Or 24 . . . R—N2; 25 RxR *ch*, KxR; 26 RxQ, PxR; 27 QxP/N5 and White has an easy win.

25   QxQ   Resigns

If 25 . . . PxQ; 26 R—R3 mate!

This game is a wonderful object lesson in the exploitation of the difficulties arising from neglect of the center.

Morphy's utilization of the King Bishop file is striking in its simplicity; but even more impressive to the student is the fact that the whole attack, powerful as it is, stems from the basic stratagem of *opening a line of attack by means of a Pawn exchange.*

CHAPTER 23

How Superior Mobility Leads to Line-opening

Alexander Alekhine was the most brilliant player in the history of chess, but in the following game we observe his masterly skill at encirclement strategy.

The setting is much the same as in the last three chapters: Black neglects the center, gets a poor development and a cramped game. But instead of striving for a brilliant refutation, Alekhine methodically drives back the enemy forces until no halfway playable course is left to Black.

Once that Black has been reduced to virtual immobility, Alekhine casts about for a method of opening new lines. As in Chapter 22, *this is accomplished by Pawn moves*. The difference is that Morphy opened the King Bishop file and obtained a King-side attack, while Alekhine opens the Queen Bishop file and utilizes that line for infiltration on the Queen-side.

You are invited to admire Alekhine's remarkable 7 P—QR4 !— a far-sighted prelude to his intended encirclement strategy. Such moves are unthinkable in the games of an amateur; but the master has years of experience in similar situations to guide him along the lines he must pursue to give the game its appropriate conclusion.

KING FIANCHETTO DEFENSE
FOLKESTONE, 1933

WHITE	BLACK
Dr. A. Alekhine	V. Mikenas
1 P—Q4	P—KN3

247

This move immediately gives us a clue to the coming proceedings. Black does not seem to care about getting a foothold
in the center.

By playing 1 . . . P—Q4 or 1 . . . N—KB3, Black would
prevent his opponent from setting up a broad center by 2 P—
K4. White seizes the proffered opportunity with:

2   P—K4   B—N2

DIAGRAM 193

(after 2 . . . B—N2)
Black is destined to have a
cramped position.

True, Black's Bishop strikes along the long diagonal (KR1—
QR8); but Black's pieces cannot function in the center, which
has been preempted by White. Just what this means will become clear to you as the game continues.

Compare the position of the Black Bishop in this diagram by
the way with the position of the same Bishop in the Dragon
Variation (see page 64, for example). Here the Bishop stares
uselessly at an amply protected Pawn; *in the Dragon Variation
the fianchettoed Bishop is powerful because Black has taken
steps to minimize the power of White's Pawn center by quickly
removing White's Queen Pawn!*

3   N—QB3   P—Q3

Black is afraid to play the natural developing move . . . N—KB3 as the Knight can simply be kicked back by 4 P—K5.

He therefore resorts to the text as a timid preparation for trying to gain a foothold in the center by . . . P—K4. That is to say, he has to strive laboriously for what White has achieved effortlessly—getting Pawns on the fourth rank! Again and again we see how the future course of the game will shape up: White's position is free and his pieces come out effortlessly; Black's position is cramped and his development is slow, strained, unwieldy, ineffective.

4	N—B3	N—Q2
5	B—QB4	....

The Bishop is developed to a very effective square, from which it aims at Black's weak point KB2.

Black must now decide whether he wants to play the move at which all his strategy has been directed thus far: 5 . . . P—K4. The drawback to the move is that it does nothing to break White's pressure on the weak point KB2 which is exercised by his Bishop at QB4.

DIAGRAM 194

(after 5 B—QB4)
White's King Bishop has a powerful diagonal.

5 . . . .   P—K3

Obviously deciding to break the diagonal of White's Bishop on QB4.

The tactical considerations are interesting, for if 5 . . . P—K4?; 6 BxP ch !, KxB; 7 N—N5 ch. If now 7 . . . K—B3?; 8 N—Q5 mate! ! If 7 . . . K—B1?; 8 N—K6 ch wins the Queen!

There remains only 7 . . . K—K1 (7 . . . K—K2; 8 N—Q5 ch is worse for Black); 8 N—K6, Q—K2; 9 N—Q5, Q—B2 *; 10 N/Q5xP ch (10 N/K6xP ch is also good) and Black's game is in a hopeless state.

6   Castles   . . . .

White's lead in development, quantitatively and qualitatively, becomes ever more noticeable. White has brought out three pieces and castled, putting his King in perfect safety and creating the possibility of posting his King Rook effectively in due course.

Black, on the other hand, has a cramped, slow development with no prospects of improvement—where is his Queen Bishop to move? ?—and his King has just had a narrow escape.

6   . . . .   N—K2

The natural move is 6 . . . KN—B3, but then there is always the danger that P—K5 will drive the Knight away.

Hence Black must again content himself with a second-rate developing move: . . . N—K2 instead of . . . KN—B3.

Because Black has already committed himself to a definite type of position, White can forecast his future strategy for the remainder of the game.

Black has developed his forces on the second and third ranks and is condemned to a permanently cramped position. His Queen Bishop, one may confidently anticipate, will never have a good square. The same thought applies to his Queen and to his Rooks.

* If 9 . . . QxN; 10 NxP ch wins the Queen. For similar examples of the fork see *Winning Chess*, p. 29.

DIAGRAM 195

(after 6 . . . N—K2)
Black is already intimidated!

Our key thought, then, is that *Black will remain constricted throughout the coming play.* White's first objective is to reduce his opponent to utter helplessness; his second thought, to exploit Black's inability to fight back when the decisive point is reached.

7 P—QR4 !   . . . .

Apparently very puzzling, but not really so if you know White's plan. This is the way he reasons: White's preponderance in development and in space on the King-side and in the center is such that if Black is to free himself, it can only be on the Queen-side. Such an attempt might come in the form of . . . P—QB3 and . . . P—QN4, gaining space on the Queenside for developing the Queen Bishop (. . . B—N2), the Queen (. . . Q—B2), freeing himself a bit (. . . N—N3), advancing in the center (. . . P—Q4) and initiating a general Pawn advance (. . . P—QR4 and . . . P—N5) which might open a file on the Queen-side and thus put Black's Rooks in business in a big way.

Of course this might not get Black very far; it might be nothing more, ultimately, then a demonstration rather than real counterplay. Yet it would lead to a real game, a real struggle.

However, by playing P—QR4 White stifles all these chances of counterplay from the very start. *This illustrates the importance of following a logical plan.*

	7	Castles
	8 B—K3	P—KR3

Black views with distaste the possibility of White's playing 9 Q—Q2 followed by 10 B—KR6 removing the valuable fianchettoed Bishop who is the chief guardian of the otherwise weak black squares on the King-side.

	9 Q—Q2	K—R2

DIAGRAM 196

(after 9 . . . K—R2)
White continues his encirclement strategy.

	10 P—R3 !	. . . .

This by no means obvious move is the kind of continuation that one cannot find unless one is actually following a plan.

As part of his "encirclement" strategy, White intends to answer . . . N—KB3 with P—K5, driving the Knight away. But without White's last move, Black could answer . . . N—N5, attacking White's King Pawn and also threatening . . . NxB. (This last is a threat in the sense that any attempt by Black to free himself must be considered a threat.)

To sum up, after 10 P—R3 ! it is pointless for Black to try
to post his Queen Knight more aggressively, 10 . . . N—KB3
being answered by the aggressive and constricting 11 P—K5.

10 . . . .   P—QB3

This is Black's only hope of obtaining some *Lebensraum*. But
its effect at best can only be slight, due to the timely interpolation of White's 7 P—QR4.

11   B—B4 !   . . . .

Moving the same piece twice, but with a purpose: he wants
to force a new weakness in Black's Pawn position, now that
Black's Queen Pawn is no longer guarded by a Pawn.

DIAGRAM 197

(after 11 B—B4 !)
White's pressure is beginning
to be noticeable.

Note, by the way, that White's second move with the Queen
Bishop, while a formal violation of the rules of good development, is actually no great crime. White has such an enormous
lead in development that he can indulge in some waste, especially when he monopolizes the center as well. (Observe that
Black's Knights cannot move to any square on the fourth
rank.)

11 . . . .   P—Q4

At last, after a great deal of twisting and arduous prepara‧
tion, Black finally gets a foothold in the center—which, how‧
ever, he could have had without any suffering on the very first
move! !

DIAGRAM 198

(after 11 . . . P—Q4)
Black makes the advance
which would have given him
a good game on the first
move!

Thus we see that Black has finally managed to get a foothold
in the center with . . . P—Q4, but only after afflicting himself
with an inferior development which leaves him with a worth-
less game. Compare Black's position, here, for example, with
his situation in Diagram 142, which has come about after reso-
lute simplifying and determined development of his pieces on
good squares—all this *after firmly establishing himself in the
center on the very first move.*

12   B—Q3   P—R3

After this White's Queen Bishop gets a powerful post at Q6.
The alternative 12 . . . N—B3; 13 P—K5, N—K1 prevents
B—Q6, but leaves Black with a hopelessly bottled-up position.
    Slightly better was 12 . . . PxP; 13 NxP, N—Q4 when
Black's game is less constricted than after the text.

13   B—Q6   . . . .

If now 13 . . . N—B3; 14 P—K5, N—K1; 15 B—R3 and Black is tied hand and foot. Again and again this theme is repeated: *when you play according to plan, you cannot afford to forget the dominant theme for even one move.*

13 . . . .   P—KB4

DIAGRAM 199

(after 13 . . . P—KB4)
Black forces the issue—to his
sorrow.

Black's last move has behind it a certain kind of twisted logic. He wants to force White's hand. If White plays PxP, Black has a certain amount of additional maneuvering space. If, on the other hand, White plays P—K5, Black is more tied up than ever. However, by playing P—K5, White closes up lines and thus diminishes his prospects of coming to grips with Black.

And so White must choose between 14 PxP and 14 P—K5. What will his decision be?

14 P—K5 !   . . . .

White decided on the Pawn advance for a number of reasons:

(1) The fact that Black is well barricaded for the moment does not mean that he can remain strongly entrenched forever.

White has faith in his ability to find some way of exploiting the superior position of his forces.

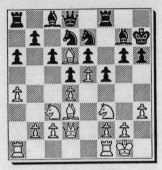

DIAGRAM 200

(after 14 P—K5 !)
The blockade of Black's game
is becoming serious.

(2) Not only do White's pieces have superior mobility; he has ways of increasing their mobility, while the same is not true of Black's pieces.

(3) The advance P—K5 assures White of the permanent posting of his mighty Queen Bishop on Q6. The dominating position of the Bishop here has a crippling effect on Black's efforts to free himself.

14   . . . .   KR—N1

Unpinning his Knight at K2. Black chafes under the restraint imposed on him.

15   P—R4   . . . .

More restraint: Black is prevented from acquiring more terrain at some time or other by . . . P—KN4.

15   . . . .   P—N3

Black is playing for the logical advance . . . P—QB4, which will give him more playing space on the Queen-side. Black nat-

urally strives, insofar as it is in his power, to resist White's
constricting policy.

16   N—K2   . . . .

DIAGRAM 201

(after 16 N—K2)
Can Black attain a modicum
of freedom by advancing his
Queen Bishop Pawn?

16   . . . .   N—B1

The indicated move was 16 . . . P—B4, cracking down on
White's center. Yet Black avoids this obvious move. Why?

The point is that 16 . . . P—B4 is refuted by 17 N—B4 at-
tacking the King Pawn. If then 17 . . . N—B1 or 17 . . . N—
N1 then 18 PxP wins a Pawn. Or if 17 . . . P—B5; 18 NxKP,
Q—K1; 19 N—B7 forking Queen and Queen Rook.*

17   P—QR5 !   . . . .

A very fine move. While Black is temporarily unable to play
. . . P—B4, White gets lasting control of the black squares on
the Queen-side by forcing the disappearance of Black's Queen
Knight Pawn from QN3. Whether Black moves his Queen
Knight Pawn or leaves it at QN3, he cannot avoid losing Pawn
control of the vital square QB4.

* For the fork, see *Winning Chess*, p. 29.

Once this Pawn control is lost, Black will never be able to
free himself with . . . P—B4; and in addition White will be
occupying this important square himself.

17 . . . .   P—QN4

As has been pointed out, neither capturing . . . PxP nor allowing White to play PxP would make any essential difference
as regards the further course of the game.

DIAGRAM 202

(after 17 . . . P—QN4)
Black no longer has any potential freeing moves.

White has made considerable progress with his encirclement
strategy. Now that the freeing advance . . . P—B4 has been
ruled out, there remains only one rather slight hope for Black:
a possible . . . P—N4 later on.

Even though this advance cannot possibly be managed now,
White nevertheless takes steps to prevent it for all time. Once
these permanent preventive measures have been taken, White
can forget about the King-side for good and turn all his attention to the Queen-side.

18	P—KN3	R—R1
19	K—N2	K—N1
20	R—R1	K—B2
21	N—B4	KR—N1

DIAGRAM 203

(after 21 . . . KR—N1)
How is White to make further
progress?

This is the most important stage of the whole game. White
determined on a plan many moves ago: to constrict Black's
position. Following up his plan consistently, White blockaded
his opponent on both wings. The consequence of this planning
procedure is that Black is helpless.

Well, what then? What does White do about it? What he
now does is the most important feature of this highly instructive game. *He opens up a line on which he can penetrate into*

DIAGRAM 204

(after 22 P—N3 *!*)
White plans to open the
Queen Bishop file.

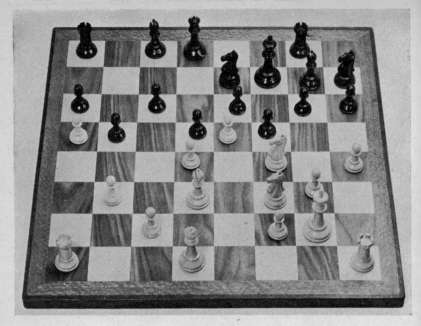

Figure 17

White has advanced the Queen Knight Pawn in order to open a file and thus be in a position to penetrate into Black's cramped formation. Here again we see the importance of line-opening *through Pawn capture, in this case prepared by the preliminary Pawn advances 22 P—N3 ! and 23 P—B4 !*

his opponent's position. Black's lack of mobility makes it impossible for him to meet force with force. White musters superior force, and he deploys it with superior mobility.

22   **P—N3** !   . . . .

After the explanation of White's strategy, the meaning of his advance of the Queen Knight Pawn becomes crystal-clear. The key-move here is P—B4, which will result in due course in the opening of the Queen Bishop file. This is the line on which

White will muster superior force for his successful invasion of Black's position. (*See Diagram 204.*)

22 .... N—R2

As far as the Queen-side is concerned, Black has nothing better than marking time. On the other wing, he still toys with the possibility of . . . P—N4.

23 P—B4! ....

DIAGRAM 205

(after 23 P—B4!)
White is ready to utilize the
Queen Bishop file.

Now the line-opening is inevitable. Its technical aspect is of the greatest importance to those who want to improve their game. *Line-opening comes about through Pawn captures. Therefore, when you want to open lines of attack, you create opportunities for Pawn captures.*

23 .... B—Q2
24 QR—QB1 ....

White can double Rooks on the Queen Bishop file if he wants to, or has to; Black cannot imitate this maneuver.

White can bring a Knight to the magnificent outpost square QB5. Black cannot imitate this maneuver.

Thus we see that White has all the solid, favorable, promising possibilities that are contained in the position. All this comes about from Black's poor opening and White's well-planned exploitation of it.

24	....	B—KB1
25	B—K2 !	....

A very fine move. Its most obvious point is that it prepares for the powerful maneuver N—Q3—B5.

DIAGRAM 206

(after 25 B—K2 !)
White makes room for N—Q3.

Suppose that Black makes a desperate attempt to get some air by (finally) playing 25 . . . P—N4. Then there comes 26 RPxP, NxP; 27 NxN *ch*, PxN; 28 B—R5 *ch*, K—N2; 29 NxP *ch !*, BxN; 30 QxP *ch* followed by mate. Or if 27 . . . RxN; 28 N—R3, KR—N1; 29 B—R5 *ch*, K—N2; 30 N—B4 and Black's game is desperate indeed.

(*We return now to the position of Diagram 206.*)

25	....	N—B1
26	BPxQP !	....

Opening the all-important Queen Bishop file.

26	....	BPxP

DIAGRAM 207

(after 26 BPxP)
At last—the opening of the
Queen Bishop file!

It will not do to play 26 . . . NxB or 26 . . . BxB, for then
27 PxP *ch*, BxP; 28 NxB, KxN; 29 RxP results in a disastrous
pin * for Black.

27	BxB	NxB
28	R—B5	....

White proceeds systematically to monopolize the open file.

28	....	N—QR2
29	N—Q3	....

The Knight will land on QB5 in due course. (*See Diagram
208.*)

White's strategy is clearly mapped out for him. He will set
up a stranglehold on the Queen Bishop file; he will occupy the
weak black squares which Black cannot guard adequately; he
will reduce Black's mobility more and more; he will bring pressure to bear on Black's weak King Pawn and Queen Rook
Pawn.

29	....	K—N2

29 . . . P—N4 would merely permit White to seize another
open file: 30 PxP etc.

* For the pin, see *Winning Chess*, p. 7.

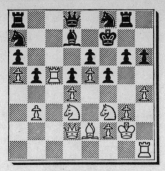

DIAGRAM 208

(after 29 N—Q3)
The Knight heads for QB5.

30 KR—QB1   . . . .

Having in view some such continuation as R—B7 followed by Q—N4 and Q—Q6. Black tries to dispute the open file.

30 . . . .   R—B1
31 RxR   BxR

If 31 . . . NxR; 32 N—B5 wins the Queen Rook Pawn!

32 Q—B3 !   . . . .

DIAGRAM 209

(after 32 Q—B3 !)
Now the Queen uses the Queen Bishop file as a highway.

The exchange of Rooks has not relieved Black's congestion appreciably. White retains his stranglehold on the Queen Bishop file and is now ready to increase the pressure until Black reaches the breaking point.

32	....	K—R2
33	Q—B5 !	R—N2
34	Q—N6 !	....

DIAGRAM 210

(after 34 Q—N6 !)
The encirclement makes rapid
progress now.

The noose gets tighter and tighter around Black's neck. If now 34 . . . QxQ ?; 35 PxQ wins a piece!

| 34 | .... | Q—K2 |
| 35 | N—B5 | .... |

Note the repeated occupation of this important square. Black's Queen Rook Pawn must now be lost, which is enough to decide the fate of the game.

Black therefore resorts to a desperate demonstration on the other wing. He has nothing more to lose, come what may.

35	....	P—N4
36	PxP	PxP
37	N—K1 !	....

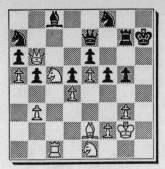

DIAGRAM 211

(after 37 N—K1 !)
Black's "attack" is stymied.

How is Black to continue his "attack"? If 37 . . . P—N5; 38
N/K1—Q3 followed by 39 N—B4 with enhanced pressure on
Black's weak Pawn. If 37 . . . P—B5; 38 B—N4 again with
enhanced pressure on the weak King Pawn.

(*We return now to the position of Diagram 211.*)

37	. . . .	N—N3
38	N/K1—Q3	P—B5
39	R—R1 *ch*	K—N1
40	B—N4 !	PxP
41	PxP	. . . .

DIAGRAM 212

(after 41 PxP)
The encirclement is complete!

White has completed a masterpiece of encirclement. If now 41 . . . N—B1; 42 R—R6 and White makes sure of picking up the weak King Pawn before he confiscates the Rook Pawn as well.

There is something very satisfying in seeing how consistently and thoughtfully White has held to his original plan of the game, which might be summed up in the following phases:

(1) Black condemns himself to a cramped position.

(2) White hits on the strategical plan of steadily constricting Black's game.

(3) White follows through systematically to execute this plan.

(4) Having achieved his strategical objective, White casts about for a way of opening new lines by means of Pawn captures.

(5) First he plays P—QN3 and P—QB4, leading to the opening of the Queen Bishop file.

(6) Then White masses his forces on this open line, utilizing it as a springboard for invading Black's position.

(7) By means of another capture (PxP in reply to . . . P—KN4) he obtains control of the King Rook file as soon as it is opened. In this way he enhances his threats against Black's vulnerable weaknesses.

(*We return now to the position of Diagram 212.*)

| 41 | . . . . | N—R5 *ch* |

This sacrifice is quite hopeless, and therefore incomprehensible to the uninitiated.

But as we know that the secret of White's success lies in the occupation of newly-opened lines, we know that the "logical" or "reasonable" 41 . . . N—B1 is smashed by 42 R—R6 (play on the open file). Realizing that he is lost, Black gives a spite check which has no more significance than an impotent flare of temper.

| 42 | PxN | PxP |

43	N—B2	R—B2
44	NxKP	K—R2
45	Q—Q6	Resigns

Black is a piece down without the slightest compensation. White's relentless execution of a brilliant plan makes this game a thing of enchantment to anyone who studies it in detail. Such games are even more beautiful than the most sparkling sacrifices!

About the Authors

I. A. HOROWITZ, *editor and publisher of Chess Review since 1933, has been one of America's outstanding chessmasters for more than twenty years. He has won the United States Open Championship three times, and he played on the winning American teams in the International Team Tournaments at Prague, 1931; Warsaw, 1935; and Stockholm, 1937.*

FRED REINFELD *is credited with being the world's most prolific chess writer. He has also defeated many of America's leading masters in international competition. After annexing the Intercollegiate Championship in his undergraduate days, he won the New York State Championship twice and subsequently became the titleholder of both the Marshall and Manhattan Chess Clubs.*